Teaching on a Tightrope

The Diverse Roles
of a Great Teacher

Jack Zevin

ROWMAN & LITTLEFIELD EDUCATION
A division of
ROWMAN & LITTLEFIELD PUBLISHERS, INC.
Lanham • New York • Toronto • Plymouth, UK

Frontispiece: "The Lecture" (1695) attributed to Wm. Hogarth. Owned by the author.

Published by Rowman & Littlefield Education
A division of Rowman & Littlefield Publishers, Inc.
A wholly owned subsidiary of
The Rowman & Littlefield Publishing Group, Inc.
4501 Forbes Boulevard, Suite 200, Lanham, Maryland 20706
http://www.rowmaneducation.com

Estover Road, Plymouth PL6 7PY, United Kingdom

British Library Cataloguing in Publication Information Available

Library of Congress Cataloging-in-Publication Data

Zevin, Jack.
  Teaching on a tightrope : the diverse roles of a great teacher / Jack Zevin.
      p. cm.
  Includes bibliographical references.
  ISBN 978-1-60709-589-7 (cloth : alk. paper) — ISBN 978-1-60709-590-3 (pbk. : alk. paper) — ISBN 978-1-60709-591-0 (electronic)
  1. Effective teacher. 2. Educational leadership. 3. Role playing. 4. Classroom management. I. Title.
  LB1025.3.Z467 2010
  371.102—dc22   2010018518

∞™ The paper used in this publication meets the minimum requirements of American National Standard for Information Sciences—Permanence of Paper for Printed Library Materials, ANSI/NISO Z39.48-1992.

Printed in the United States of America.

Contents

Preface

Even a rock can be teacher.

—Old Buddhist proverb

You are invited to consider teaching as role-play, teaching as a relationship between actress/actor and audience. Everyone teaches—presentation, explanation, instruction, pedagogy—but few think about its conception and design, its component parts, or how these add up to more than a sum of the parts.

This book is designed to assist you in thinking about the act of teaching on both sides of the desk, podium, stage, field, and even computer screen. Nowadays, in this age of postmodernism, ubiquitous cell phones, and knowledge by download, we often forget who is teaching and who is learning or why. We don't think about the theory, the metaphor, inherent in a teacher's actions. Even the teacher may be unaware of the dynamic that lies at the depths of the role.

The age-old problems of teaching and learning are still very much with us, even though many administrations, politicians, and private and government agencies are hell-bent to "reform" the "system." Government agencies and private interests set goals for what each and every child, young adult, and adult should learn. Values are demanded for becoming an adequate public citizen, a thoughtful environmentalist, and a smart shopper. Most of all, it is important not to be a drag on the workplace!

Old problems are still with us for two major reasons: First, we have a simpleminded "model" of instruction and what it is supposed to accomplish, information in and testing out. Second, we often view our audience with a mixture of contempt and/or authority that overlooks

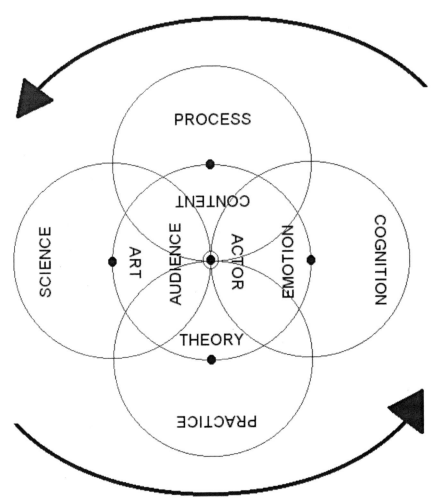

Figure P.I.   Intersections

both their strengths and weaknesses, and denies them a feeling of participation and contribution.

Many teachers—and parents, business leaders, politicians, coaches, and symphony conductors (teachers all)—act as if they believe (and probably do believe) that to teach is to learn. They view their role as to be in command and act the authority, to provide direction and answers to build appreciation and gratitude. Alas, the results of national testing, local testing, quizzes, surveys, exams, and other assessment devices often (but not always; let's be a bit hopeful!) show that input alone doesn't seem to do the trick, and can actually produce negative results in terms of student attitudes.

More is needed than the notion that teaching is communication that can deliver content efficiently and effectively. Teachers talk and talk, computers download, principals direct, and (voilà!) students learn, and understand complex material. This simpleminded idea of cause and effect leads to demands for constantly increasing test scores when it is obvious to some that the vast overload of data now available has done little to improve student performance.

Effective teachers first and foremost must build relationships between actress/actor and audience. Relationships, mediated by roles, encourage a flow of information, ideas, and feelings between and within both "sides." Actually, there really aren't two sides at all (i.e., teacher and student), but rather a duality, a dyad, in which either or both can contribute to or take away from the learning and teaching process. Teaching is an organic relationship between partners playing roles that take time to develop, with short- and long-term effects that are not always predictable.

The big idea of this book is that roles are malleable and interchangeable. Teachers can assume roles for different objectives, and so can students. Teachers and students can exchange roles as well, with the teacher playing a student, and the student playing a teacher. The many roles of a teacher can range across a wide spectrum of actions, from being a tough little Mussolini to a warmhearted anarchist. Each role has a goal, a style, and an impact. Willy-nilly, teachers impact their students in ways that are evident and direct, or indirect and delayed. And above all, we need to communicate across roles with each other.

Many teachers teach for themselves, basically overlooking audience reaction, even when adverse. They move on to other things long before their pupils have demonstrated, clearly, that the materials *were intelligently absorbed and understood.* Getting an audience to really understand and apply ideas new to them is no easy matter, even if they are motivated and interested. So let's think about those who are bored, disabled, phobic, or average, or who see little or no value in learning a lot of "stuff," old and abstract stuff.

Even worse for role-play is the problem of social status, with lower socioeconomic groups tending to perform more poorly on assessments than middle- or upper-level groups. A social problem confronts us as teachers. Not only is learning distributed along class lines, but social standing also shapes the roles that are accepted or rejected. Many groups prefer a tough disciplinarian for a teacher, though they may rebel. Others prefer more inquiry, more discussion, and debating styles of teaching because they want to participate in shaping learning themselves.

So, here we are in search of some ideas about teaching roles that might give us insights into why old ways are or are not working, and which new roles might be tried out. One of the major ideas offered in this book is the notion that audiences can teach as well as learn, and teachers can learn and listen as well as audiences. This is a rather simple idea, which many teachers avoid, deny, ignore, or give lip service to now and then.

Nevertheless, teaching permits many roles that have significant impact on student lives, permanently changing lives through knowledge, skills, and/or emotional growth. This means that we need a "paradigm shift" in thinking, away from traditional views of teacher roles as authorities. We need to think more about the teacher as a participant in an ongoing learning/instructional struggle where each partner contributes to the overall outcome. We need to rethink teaching as roles, as methods of transferring knowledge, ideas, skills, and attitudes back and forth, while pressing for growth in directions that improve individuals and promote social harmony.

There are many worthwhile topics and subjects in our curriculum, but the rationale for learning these may or may not be apparent to an audience. The topic, the process, the teacher, the curriculum, and the social setting must be integrated with students' abilities and interests if we are to succeed as teachers. We need to learn to play many roles, altering behavior to attain different goals with varying audiences. Attainment levels are all arbitrary anyway, and it is growth that really counts, providing we recognize it in ourselves and in our students.

Teacher-centered instruction should be viewed as interrelated with student-centered instruction; they should be seen as complementary roles. The teacher can be a student, or an actress, or fall in between, switching sides at will for effect, to dramatize communication (one heck of a great teacher, this!). It doesn't matter, in this view, who or what medium is delivering the information—live human, video or audio recording, or website narrator. But it does matter a great deal *how* the delivery is made—whether the audience role allows or encourages interaction with the teacher role and the material.

Sophisticated educational theory has rediscovered, revivified, and synthesized many older theories about child-centered versus teacher-centered classrooms. These theories offer views of process versus content, individualized versus social learning, lecture versus cooperative learning, and so on (Lobato 2003, 17–20; Greeno, Smith, and Moore 1993; Cobb and Bowers 1999).

Many different exciting roles are suggested for both students and teachers, including creative use of groups and shared processing of data. Some of this lovely, rediscovered theory—"design-based research" and "actor-oriented transfer"—has promoted creative classroom activities. Some has led reformers to institute a kind of top-down reshaping of vast school systems, such as New York City, in which cooperative learning comes in a standard size and is a must for all. Progressive education (John Dewey rolls over in his grave!) is reborn as institutional reform but without much of the democratic give-and-take of discussion between audience and actors.

Therefore, we must again revisit the many roles a teacher (or a student) can play in or out of class. We need to look at role models operating as teachers in many venues—sports, business, media, school, and even the military—to see who gets results that last. We need to think of ourselves as teachers who can play many roles to help our students, including student. So let's explore metaphors for roles in teaching and learning. Let's apply art and science, content and process, to our conception of instruction. Let's think about what will help us all experiment with acting and being acted upon to achieve worthwhile objectives for our audiences in many walks of life.

Acknowledgments

Over the course of a lifetime in teaching, teaching students in middle and high school, and teaching teachers how to teach, there are innumerable people to thank for influencing the formation of this book. Ideas can spring up from many sources and combine to assist thinking and rethinking of the teacher's roles in and out of classrooms. Therefore, please allow me to express my thanks to several generations of teachers and students who have suggested many of the ideas in this book. Specifically, I also need to thank my wife, Iris, a classroom teacher who often brings ethereal lesson plans down to earth and reminds me of the importance of audience. Thanks also go to a valued research assistant, Anne Marie Nava, who helped create the circles representing the intersection of ideas about teaching.

It is my wish that *Teaching on a Tightrope* will suggest antidotes to monochromatic and rigid conceptions of what teaching is all about, whether one is a parent, a boss, a coach, a leader, or, last but not least, a teacher.

I

The Five Dimensions
of Teaching Roles

My headmaster read my tablet, said:
"There is something missing," caned me. . . .

The fellow in charge of silence said:
"Why did you talk without permission," caned me.

The fellow in charge of assembly . . . said:
"Why did you 'stand at ease' without permission," caned
me.

The fellow in charge of the gate said:
"Why did you go out from (the gate) without permission,"
caned me. . . .

The fellow in charge of Sumerian said:
"Why didn't you speak Sumerian," caned me. . . .

My teacher (ummia) said:
"Your hand is unsatisfactory," caned me.

(And so) I (began to) hate the scribal art, (began to) neglect
the scribal art.
  My teacher took no delight in me; (even) (stopped teaching) me his skill in the scribal art; in no way prepared me in
the matters (essential) to the art (of being) a "young scribe,"
(or) the art (of being) a "big brother."

—Samuel Noah Kramer, *The Sumerians*[1]

In life we are all teachers, whether or not we know it. Our actions—how
we perform—depend on our goals, our situation, and our background.
Also important are the expectations and abilities of the audience, in
addition to our mood and condition. Of course, there are also higher

authorities that influence our teaching in the form of an administration, standards, regulations, theories, and the fad of the moment; and above all stands the state.

We all learned to teach from others: parents, peers, role models, coaches, schoolteachers, religious leaders, bosses—a plethora of influences. We learned content, method, style, and philosophy, consciously and subconsciously, from many human and media sources. Along the way, we acquired a teacher persona used in daily communication and conversation, both consciously and subconsciously.

In addition, we acquired teaching "methods," perhaps taken for granted without thinking too much about their implications for "learners." Methods may be based on traditions and models that we have never questioned or tested. But we continue to follow these time-honored practices because of acceptance by others. Audiences usually go along with traditional forms even where a rationale may be unclear or absent.

Many people go through the motions of what we call "teaching" but never reach their audience, or cannot tell *if* they have reached their audience. Some don't know how to read an audience or don't seem to care. Quite a few teach to and for themselves, and react very critically when audiences don't seem to get their points or are unable to remember the information conveyed. A few punish their audiences and are in turn treated badly. The atmosphere for learning can deteriorate markedly, or may be poor to begin with, yet the same methods persist!

Whether experiencing successes or failures or both, we need to reflect upon our own role and performance as teachers. Take this opportunity to think about yourself as a teacher playing many roles. While reading this book, consider the many ways you can expand and enrich your current views and practices. View your encounter with "roles" as a step toward opening up teaching to include many new ideas and techniques that you may not have thought were part of teacher behavior. Your may want to reconsider instructional methods, style, and patterns, and evaluate their impact on an audience.

REFLECTION ON THE IDEA OF TEACHING, THE MANY ROLES OF A TEACHER, IS EXACTLY WHAT THIS BOOK IS INTENDED TO BE ALL ABOUT

Questions and ideas are raised to stimulate your consideration of instructional situations, or what has been termed a "situative perspective," as Greeno (1997) calls the classroom atmosphere and setting.[2] Our situations include ourselves, of course, our students, significant others, the place and time in which we are located, the materials we are using, and the techniques or methods of delivery.[3] Situations include

1) physical and social contexts;
2) community and group experience;
3) delivery to individuals and groups through technology or in person.[4]

"Situative theorists" generally view teaching as arising out of and being part of a social and historical context. Context is based on interaction between and among different roles for the purpose of accomplishing some type of learning, providing knowledge and skills, or transmitting ideas and values (Lave and Wenger 1991). Theorists do not think of teaching as information and ideas independent of time and place. Rather, how someone learns material depends on the social setting and the techniques of presentation—factors in an overall interactive package.

Learning and teaching take place in a community where roles are laid out for actresses and actors to play. Results develop out of interchanges with others, with subject matter, with methods, and with technical tools and media (Brown 1993). The "truth" of what we are teaching at any one time, the very words we use to express it, are dependent upon myriad factors that we, as teachers, have filtered through our own personalities and experiences.

Audience, an often-overlooked factor in the teaching situation, is critically important to performance. Much depends upon its human characteristics, composition and background, enthusiasms and expectations. Whether composed of the one, the few, or the many, your audience can make or break a presentation. Most teachers "play" to their audience in some fashion, as actresses/actors or as founts of knowledge and expertise. They alter strategies along the way, depending upon their "reading" of individual and group reactions.

In relating to audiences, much depends upon the sources of a teacher's goals and philosophy. External goals usually result in treating audiences as passive or automatically receptive, while internal goals usually result in treating audiences as active and reactive. Because teaching is a complex interplay of methods, materials, delivery, and ideas, the relationship between actress/actor and audience may be greatly enhanced or inhibited by these vital factors.

For example, if you are the teacher and you have been directed to "cover" the theory of evolution today for your high-school or college audience, then your attitude will tend to be one of authority. The audience's role is to learn what is given and to be able to accurately repeat the information on a test of some sort. The teacher may approach this audience with a mind-set that the delivery of information is all-important, paying little attention to audience capabilities.

However, if you seek to inspire the learners' interpretations of evolution as a concept, then your attitude will emphasize exchange and redirection, placing a premium on audience feedback, questions, and understanding. What goals you choose as the teacher/actress/actor will strongly impact the audience and provoke a reaction. A presentation can yield very different behaviors and attitudes toward you as a person and a teacher, and toward the subject matter and method of presentation. Thus, we propose that the role you play in relationship to your audience creates a "marriage" that can produce a harmony of powerful learning, or the discordant notes of rejection and disinterest.

METAPHORS AND SIMILES TO HELP US THINK ABOUT TEACHING

We also need to consider teaching roles in terms of similes and metaphors. Teaching is teaching, whatever that covers, and it is a lot of ground to take in at one gulp! However, there are rich analogies that can be drawn between teaching and the following: parenting, sports,

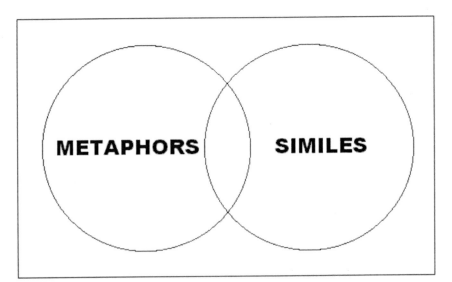

Figure 1.1. Metaphors and Similes

business, theater, performance, politics, and governing. Simply standing behind a podium or on a stage with a piece of paper in hand, delivering a memorized speech—or, better yet, using a teleprompter—distances teacher from listeners.

Telling an audience what they can just as easily read themselves or look up on the Web is not a very efficient or effective instructional approach for building understanding. Lecturing relies on an ancient storyteller model of instruction that was probably evolved for keeping oral traditions alive, and it may work well to deliver information, up to a point. However, in these days of high technology and the Internet, how effective are lectures in building comprehension of subjects? Can't we learn about ancient Egyptian history, auto-repair techniques, or anatomy online?

So why lecture? How, instead, could we use our role most productively in face-to-face instruction? On the other hand, most teachers at all levels love to talk, to lecture. College faculty, sad to say, may be among the most notable in acting out their very best or very worst to a "tell-all" performance model. Many fine professors offer a "directed narrative" metaphor playing a great authority from a podium or platform based on many sheets of lecture notes written on legal pads—even in this, the age of technology. Sometimes tell-all types of teachers may go so far as to use an overhead projector or a SMART Board to reproduce their notes and lectures. What innovation! Might the problem be aided by our wonderful new computer networks? Or is it possible for metaphor to trump machine?

Lectures can be transferred to theoretically "interactive" technology, yet the communication is all—or nearly all—one way!

We have but to "surf the Net" to find unnumbered examples of "talks" with claims for interaction that doesn't happen. Current

---

AUDIENCE PARTICIPATION

1. How many roles do you think a teacher can play?
2. Can a parent, a coach, a mechanic, or a passer-by play teacher?
3. What does it take to play a teacher's role? How can you tell?
4. Does technology solve our problems with respect to adopting teacher roles?
5. Are there any roles/metaphors that you would like to consider for your own teaching?

fashion also has "famous" faculty deliver videotaped lectures frozen in time for others to absorb and take notes on . . . or maybe forget the notes after all, since you have the video? Or maybe even forget the ideas and just watch? Or maybe sell these to drivers and couch potatoes who want to improve their memory banks for new subjects?

Perhaps the reflections and questions in this book will help us to consider alternatives to these rather limited views of the art and science of teaching as one-way communication from authority to audience.

GOALS AND OBJECTIVES

In our search for pleasing instructional metaphors and roles, the following goals will be pursued:

1. Defining *quality instruction* as an invitation to your own reflections and reactions about teaching as art and science, content and process, theory and practice, or cognition and emotion.
2. Building models of instruction to explain why some teachers (often with very different styles and personae) seem to have a great impact on audiences, while others are rejected, disliked, or avoided.
3. Comparing classroom practice with research findings to help you improve and expand the horizons of instruction.
4. Debating teacher roles in an age of well-advertised and widely disseminated technological tools and much-touted educational "progress."
5. Assessing teaching roles as practice and performance along a scale from memory and information, conformity and authority, to higher-order intellectual, creative, and ethical choices.
6. Taking a stand on whether the best teaching can be justified *when and only when* there are clear and present signals from an audience/students/learners that they are interested in paying attention.

This book, therefore, seeks to define, reflect upon, and recast the idea of teaching as metaphor and performance. We seek to implement styles of teaching that maximize student engagement with higher-level thinking. We live in an era of rising educational standards. The government and the public (occasionally) laud and (mostly) criticize teachers, schools, and educational institutions quite freely. Therefore, we need to reconsider and defend a conception of and criteria for effective, good, great, and "brilliant" teaching. And it is important that our criteria are not simply tied to knowledge memorization, regurgitation, and higher test scores.

We need to view instruction holistically as well as through its parts, much in the spirit of the old bromide "The whole is greater than the sum of the parts." Do we want to project leadership mainly through authority, providing clear and definite answers to questions and problems? Do we seek to project a predominantly "democratic" leadership style in which participation is a vital part of open questions and answers? Do we want to tailor our practices and teaching tools to an audience, or follow a "one size fits all" strategy and curriculum that everyone must attain and exceed?

There are several pivotal decision points for those who hope to play the role of actor/actress/teacher. A "democratic" classroom, as compared against an "authoritative" classroom, will take on very different dimensions and develop a very different aura. Teachers try to do both, attempting a difficult and dizzying balancing act, like a trapeze artist. Teachers can totter on a tightrope between competing philosophies and subject-matter lobbies. They are prey to vastly different conceptions of teaching and achievement that throw them off balance.

A concept of teaching must take into account both intentions and behavior, personality and methodology, art and science. A fine teacher needs a philosophy and method to hold on to through fads and pressures. Each decision is a pivotal point in your thinking about metaphors of teaching that has personal consequences for your treatment of audiences. What constitutes the act and process of teaching, and how we can categorize, rate, and judge instructional prowess, are open questions for reflection and debate. And these are important questions, the answers to which will shape our definition of a teacher's role. Your choice of roles will shape current and future relationships with those who play student to your teacher.

A MODEL FOR THINKING ABOUT TEACHING

To help spur reflection, a model of teaching *as deeply interactive* will be provided. This model is based on seeing roles as evolving relationships between a person or persons playing the role of instructor(s), and others playing the roles of students. In terms of the model, it is the role behavior that is crucial rather than the label. Many can play teacher or student, actress or audience, switching roles at will if they understand how to manage the alteration. Parents, leaders, coaches, directors, principals, gurus, police, politicians, and many others play the role of teacher. Children, followers, viewers, fans, worshippers, and teams play the role of audience.

However, a role can be learned and practiced in many different ways. So it is quite possible for people to play both audience and action roles, often simultaneously. Teaching and learning can therefore be viewed as a question of "altered states" in which borders can be crossed and recrossed without a passport. Performance is usually expressed in the form of verbal communication. However, practice can include body language, props, exhibits, demonstrations, technology, and theater. Actions and reactions should form the basis for evolving an overview of teaching as role-play, rather than prescription.

Teacher-student, actress/actor-audience relationships can be found in *all* settings, expressed through a variety of metaphors! This includes the home, the office, the sports arena, the market, the government, and the classroom. Teaching goes on almost continuously, in many venues, often quite unnoticed or unexpected. People will be playing out audience and actress/actor roles to promote learning of some kind.

This could just as easily apply to driver training, culinary arts, coaching on the field, the president's address to the nation, or a soliloquy of a famous stage artist using some famous playwright's words. Wasn't Shakespeare teaching us something through his plays, or was it simply entertainment? Aren't television chefs old and new such as Julia Child or Emeril Lagasse teaching while entertaining? (Do you remember the recipes or the performance more?)

Finally, throughout this work, let's try to avoid educational dichotomies, such as lecture versus discussion, traditional versus Socratic, teacher centered versus student centered, or process versus content. Rather, let's seek to portray teaching as one important part of a greater whole, a larger context of learning and change. Teaching may, for example, be viewed *as a dynamic "model" or set of at least five interlocking and overlapping dimensions.* These dimensions contribute to, alter, build, or inhibit student/audience engagement and the feedback that shapes learning and leads to understanding and choices.

Briefly, these five factors or dimensions (illustrated below) are

1) actor and audience
2) theory and practice
3) process and content
4) art and science
5) cognition and emotion

As you can see, each "set" or factor overlaps the others in a series of combinations that are interlocking. This is a kind of "Zen" holistic conception of teaching, a view of roles as interconnected to each other and to learning. Each set is a reflection on instructional roles connected to and drawing from many factors and elements, whether at home, on the classroom stage, in the workplace, on the playing field, or in a theater.[5]

For example, when teaching and learning as both cognition and emotion come together in a dynamic way, there is a feeling of accomplishment, personal growth, and mental stimulation. As many dimensions come together in a situation, students experience moments of gestalt, "Eureka!" or the "aha!" phenomenon.

As long as communication is presumed to be taking place *between* two or more parties, the Web, recordings, videos, and other media can serve as exchanges between teachers and students just as in classroom performance. The key is that subject matter, understanding, and emotions are being sent and received through roles shared *by at least two or more parties* simultaneously. Each party must continually diagnose, "read" each other in an attempt to understand what is expected and accomplished. Then the result will be satisfying to both rather than only one.

Contrary to the popular dictum about gender, the world's oldest profession really must be teaching. Can there possibly be any older profession, since it is through instruction that we humans learn skills and acquire knowledge? Perhaps the "first teacher" followed a trial-and-error method from personal experience? Have there always been people in the role of teacher, those acting, and others in the roles of learners, the audience?

Our Sumerian example quoted at the start of this chapter indicates a clear line of authority and order. There are signs of audience rebellion, quite recognizable to us even after four or five thousand years. Sometimes those roles can switch, with the teacher learning from the students. Those persons, the teachers, had a store of knowledge, skills, and experiences that they handed down to the next generation, with or against their active participation. Teaching took place by direct explanation and discussion, or indirectly through moralizing and storytelling.

Often, instruction was given added authority by a teacher's role that may have carried religious, civic, parental, peer, artistic and aesthetic, warrior, or athletic connotations and associations. For instance, many of those greatly beloved and honored teachers whose names come down to us from the past, such as Confucius, Jesus, Moses,

Socrates, John Dewey, Elizabeth Cady Stanton, and Martin Luther King, Jr., were religious, literary, and philosophical figures. And let's not forget the Oracle of Delphi, either!

Teacher/actress/actor is to be thought of primarily as a *role*, one that embodies a set of performance skills. The teacher is *not* simply a categorical definition, or an individual personality. In our journey of inquiry we may consider as teachers those who also occupy roles as parents, rabbis, priests, students, children, politicians, police, rock and rap stars, storytellers, journalists, attorneys, athletes, and others. In short, a wide range of people in many jobs may perform as teachers. They may also play audiences as individuals, groups, or even nations, receiving messages from others directly or through media acting in an instructional capacity.

A formal school classroom is the most commonplace location for education. While a classroom setting is not the only place where instruction occurs, it is formally, socially designated for educational purposes, with its own special advantages and constraints. Our five-part model illustrates areas of constraint and advantage, separation and fusion.

The roles of actress/actor and audience/students form the nucleus of an atom around which many electrons are whirling. This "atomic" model of teaching roles is an apt metaphor because so much is swirling around us when we teach. The path of electrons makes the outcome not entirely predictable even by the most sophisticated quantum physics. As teachers, we are all inside Heisenberg's "uncertainty principle."

We can control a good deal of what is happening, and set nice goals. But the end product is always more random than the terms set out by our plan. Teaching roles will be discussed as connected over-

---

AUDIENCE PARTICIPATION

1. Does the model work for you in describing and categorizing teaching roles?
2. Why or why not?
3. Are there other models you would like to propose?
4. How do teachers you have grown up with in elementary and secondary school fit or not fit the proposed model?
5. What roles do college teachers play for you?
6. Which teachers have you known who can fit many or all of the dimensions?

lapping dimensions composed of theory and practice, art and science, process and content, and cognition and emotion, swirling around the epicenter of actress/actor and audience.

TESTING THE MODEL BY MEETING SOCRATES

Socrates, who lived and taught in ancient Athens, a cradle of democracy, had a very distinct and critical style, at least as represented in dialogues by his pupil Plato.

We really have no direct recordings of Socrates at work, nor do we have any feedback in the form of tests, "accountable talk," or essays from his students. As represented by Plato, Socrates fills quite a few of the dimensions in our model. Preferring a one-on-one encounter with students, Socrates dealt at most with a few very active respondents. No big, inner-city classes of thirty plus for Socrates! A portion of a dialogue is quoted below, a typical argument, if you can call it that, between Socrates and Meno, a favorite of his to manipulate. Meno, you will observe, has a good deal less to say about anything than his teacher. Socrates tends to dominate the discussion, leading us to worry, perhaps, that he is not very Socratic, but rather is leading the student to a foregone conclusion.

> Socrates: And thus we arrive at the conclusion that virtue is either wholly or partly wisdom?
>
> Meno: I think that what you are saying, Socrates, is very true.
>
> Socrates: But if this is true, then the good are not by nature good?
>
> Meno: I think not.
>
> Socrates: If they had been, there would assuredly have been discerners of characters among us who would have known our future great men; and on their showing we should have adopted them, and when we had got them, we should have kept them in the citadel out of the way of harm, and set a stamp upon them far rather than upon a piece of gold, in order that no one might tamper with them; and when they grew up they would have been useful to the state?
>
> Meno: Yes, Socrates, that would have been the right way.
>
> Socrates: But if the good are not by nature good, are they made good by instruction?
>
> Meno: There appears to be no other alternative, Socrates. On the supposition that virtue is knowledge, there can be no doubt that virtue is taught.

Socrates: Yes, indeed, but what if the supposition is erroneous?

Meno: I certainly thought just now that we were right.

Socrates: Yes, Meno, but a principle which has any soundness should stand firm not only just now, but always.

Meno: Well, and why are you so slow of heart to believe that knowledge is virtue?

Socrates: I will try and tell you why, Meno. I do not retract the assertion that if virtue is knowledge it may be taught; but I fear I have some reason in doubting whether virtue is knowledge. Consider now and say whether virtue, and not only virtue but the thing that is taught, must not have teachers and disciples?

Meno: Surely.

Socrates: And conversely, may not the art of which neither teacher nor disciples exist be assumed to be incapable of being taught?

Meno: True, but do you think there are no teachers of virtue?

Socrates: I have certainly often enquired whether there were any, taken great pains to find them, and have never succeeded; and many have assisted me in the search, and they were the persons whom I thought the most likely to know . . .

He [Meno] desires to attain that kind of wisdom and virtue by which men order the state or the house, and honor their parents, and know when to receive and when to send away citizens and strangers, as a good man should. Now, to whom should he go in order that he may learn his virtue? . . .

The question is whether they were also good teachers of their own virtue—not whether they are, or have been, good men in this part of the world, but whether virtue can be taught . . . Do we mean to say that the good men of our own and of other times knew how to impart to others that virtue which they had themselves, or is virtue a thing incapable of being communicated or imparted by one man to another?[6]

As you can gather, Socrates leads and dominates this discussion, pushing poor Meno around so the answers and questions lead up to a conclusion Socrates is desirous of drawing. There is little real questioning or opposition from Meno, and the dialogue as a whole follows a very logical syllogistic model of reasoning, although there are tinges of emotion. It is certainly not without value judgments; rather, these abound on both people and arguments, and lead to the rather pessimistic conclusion that virtue cannot be taught—or can it?

But is it really an open question, or has Socrates already made a decision, leading Meno into a logical trap of agreement? This is certainly not cooperative learning as such, since the teacher is dominating the outcome, but it is not in the form of direction or lecture. Socrates' practice is inquiry, but he has a clear and definite agenda in terms of style, goals, and outcomes. Surely, our brief inquiry has demonstrated that the style of a teacher, his or her practice, may take a form that to outward appearances is student friendly and sharing, but that actually is leading to a conclusion based on a planned objective that is attained by reasoning together rather than lecture, but with the learning that occurs nonetheless remaining almost entirely one-sided. Don't you agree?

As you review the five components or dimensions of the model, think about where a Socratic dialogue fits into the scheme. How many dimensions does the dialogue inhabit and move through, and is there an equal or unequal relationship between student and teacher, actress/actor and audience?

THE FIVE COMPONENT DIMENSIONS (AN ATOMIC VIEW)

Each of the five dimensions or components presents two related dimensions of teaching. Think about each dimension in visual and kinetic terms. View the relationships in your mind's eye as overlapping and interactive. Each circle is a center with movement around it, much as atomic particles move dynamically around the nucleus of an atom.

Some particles may move regularly, others erratically, but all work together. Occasionally, however, the atom may disintegrate and all or most of the particles fly off in various directions, losing their attachment to the center. This can happen in teaching as well, so we need to keep track of the dimensions and their relationship to the center. We try as teachers to balance the different factors in our overall concept of teaching. Otherwise, we lose our role, and our audience drifts away from our teaching. Familiar?

Actress/Actor-Audience . . . Teacher-Student

Defining a teaching role is a major issue for an actress/actor, along with the concomitant problem of understanding and "reading" an audience. Central to audience/actor relationships is the question of mo-

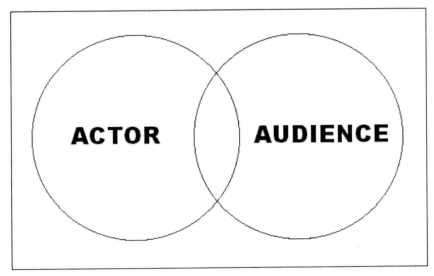

Figure 1.2.   Actor and Audience

tivation and engagement: when, how, and why a group, a class, a set of individuals can be drawn into a learning/study process. Each teacher/ actress/actor projects a subject, a method, a personality, and a message. Each attempts to match audience ability and activate audience interest. In the age-old effort to promote learning, change behavior, and develop our offspring, we seek to promote interest in learning. Audiences may be drawn in by a system of rewards and/or punishments composed of extrinsic and intrinsic motivations. In effect a teacher is a persuader if not a salesperson.

A teacher constantly seeks to build and reinforce the instructional relationship. Often, the teacher acts as the authority or, through "outside" authoritative sources, attempts to communicate established knowledge, skills, and values. The curriculum is usually set by some government agency and built into a program of study. However, delivery still depends on the teacher. The teacher is the one assigned to impart this "knowledge and virtue" to some intended audience. Success is often measured by audience performance and feedback, either formal or informal, by testing or diagnosing reactions.

Goals or outcomes are usually planned in advance for, by, and sometimes even with students. Basic to corroborating learning are answers to questions, or results on tests and examinations. In contrast to the role of authority, an actress/actor/teacher may also act as a "democratic" leader whose role is to foster discussion and debate in which students actively participate. Outcomes and results may be "negotiated" or altered by interaction with an audience who have a role in shaping direction and identifying conclusions.

A pivotal choice exists between the authoritative and the democratic roles. This decision deeply influences every aspect and dimension of all subsequent instruction.

Theory and Practice

A strong influence on all actor/actress/teacher roles (and student roles as well) is the theory (or theories) of instruction that teachers believe in and act upon. Theories are usually drawn from philosophy and psychology, serving as guides to practice, to actual performance. Choices of learning theories can also predict teaching behavior, since these may suggest ways of relating to audiences and conform to an underlying educational philosophy.

Theories of teaching may be based on personal experiences, by upbringing and background, or by contact with role models at home, schools, or jobs. Ideas may also be drawn from the cultural and social setting in which we live, more democratic or more authoritarian. In other words, all of us playing a teacher role have consciously and subconsciously adopted principles or operating rules, that is, a "theory" that guides acts of instruction.

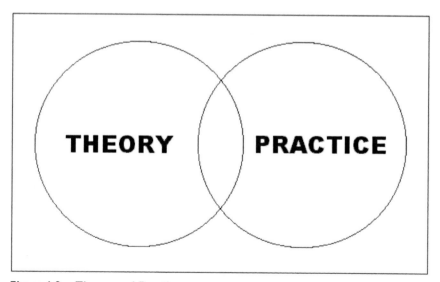

Figure 1.3.   Theory and Practice

The culture in which we are raised and educated nearly always has a profound influence on thinking about the role of teaching. For example, theoretically, in a republic with a democratic culture, teaching roles will be viewed as supportive of basic rights such as freedom of expression. Youth, potential future voters and participants in democratic cultures, need to be socialized as "good citizens" who will take active leadership roles.

However, as we all know, youths are minors, and schools seldom follow a consistent theory of either organization or instruction. Rather, there are usually competing concepts and problems. The issue of control within school culture, and personal leadership preferences of an administration, may produce greater or lesser control, more or less justification of authority. This results in a "classroom atmosphere" that may vary greatly from room to room, building to building, or system to system.

A school may closely resemble a well-organized military encampment or a town-hall meeting. However, the two models don't necessarily mesh well or promote the same kind of learning. Any philosophy of education can be interpreted quite differently by role-players—whether teachers, school leaders, parents, students, or citizens. The audience may not always agree with or view positively what the adult leadership has chosen as the primary goals. Many schools therefore suffer conflicting goals and roles, producing mixed outcomes.

Thus, contradictions and confusion may develop, with an administration spouting approval for "democratic principles" but enforcing a set of "top-down" rules. Little or no participation by teachers or students may actually be allowed in the decision-making process. A theory like Howard Gardner's "multiple intelligences" or cooperative learning may be in vogue, yet promulgated and communicated in such a way that its application is rigid and propagandistic.[7] However aggressive the administration, we still need to think for ourselves as teachers in order to derive practices that work with our student audience.

Theories of instruction and learning can be chosen because of a teacher's respect for tradition, personality, or personal preferences and style. Choices may be a result of studies drawn from educational and psychological research. Theories such as mnemonics, stimulus-response psychology, or inquiry-discovery-reflective pedagogy do influence an instructor's daily behavior. The way teachers relate to learners, the techniques to deliver information, and ideas about subject matter all reflect choices of theory (Greene 1978). In other words, our notions of good teaching strongly influence daily practice, shaping relationships between actors and audiences.

Art and Science

Practice describes the everyday classroom behavior of teachers for their audiences. This practice derives from theory based on educational research and/or philosophy, and is demonstrated in routines, as well as highly personal actions.[8] Questioning skills, homework assignments, materials selected, joking and humor, reward and punishment, directions, lectures, and discussion form practice. Each little act, every choice, from the way in which students are called upon, and in what order, to the design for a year-long course of study, is part of the art of performance. The expression of personality as living performance is part of practice, whether stage-managed or natural. Teachers, in effect, shape the material and methods to our own purposes and roles, and give it all a touch and tone that make each unique to the world of instruction, a distinct person in the eyes of our audiences.

Artistry in the classroom, as defined and acted out by teachers, may shape everyday habits. From the beginning each day, practice is demonstrated by a list of goals on the blackboard—for example, starting every lesson with a motivation or "grabber" that wakes up the audience. A teacher's view of practice may be influenced by one or more "artistic" views of instruction (Greene 1978), including staging and characterization, script writing, and building a personal relation to an audience. A teacher might display touches of hyperbole and satire, "signature" comments, provocative questions, and a distinctive style of delivery.

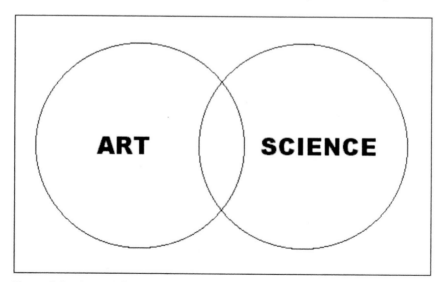

Figure 1.4.   Art and Science

Daily practice may also be formal and tightly organized around distinctive goals set by textbooks and state curricula, or more subject to teacher design. There could be predictable routines that structure every period, unit, course, and program, or there may be spontaneous emotions and debates. *Artistry* in teaching may be defined as the extent to which teachers select practices that differentiate roles, dramatize material, and ignite affection for a subject or topic. The artistic role enhances personal impact and identity upon an audience.

A *science* of instruction, by contrast, is usually taken largely from educational research and educational psychology. A science of instruction draws upon findings from psychology and "best practice" studies based upon well-established principles, scholarly thinking, and corroborated, field-tested research. This knowledge is based on conclusions articulated in public journals by experts, based on studies conducted and verified under both laboratory and field conditions—and not simply local custom or tradition.

Whatever a teacher's personality and style, favorite theory and particular practices, all components should work together to create a role, purpose, and philosophy in the eyes of the audience. Every teacher playing a role must combine artistry and science in some way, though one side or the other is given greater value.

Content and Process

The methods and techniques that make up our teacher roles are at the heart of a process of communication and delivery. *Process* incorporates elements of group dynamics, implying a relationship between teacher, audience, performance, and knowledge. Process may be lecturing, questioning, cooperative learning, discussion, debate, simulation gaming, or role-play. The choice of a process is frequently dictated by theory, by audience, and by subject matter, as well as by personal "artistic" preferences.

For example, a teacher might view an audience as greatly in need of stimulation and participation. Therefore, an active and engaging method would be preferred over one that assumes a passive role on the part of the audience. If the school atmosphere is what might be termed democratic and innovative, the teacher will choose a role-play or simulation game, perhaps, one that draws an entire class into the process. On the other hand, the teacher could have inherited the task of covering a large quantity of material, like an entire energy unit for science in time for students to take a standardized test. In this case,

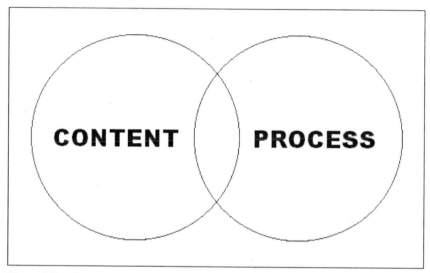

Figure 1.5.   Content and Process

lecture and review might be viewed as the most practical and efficient method of presentation.

Within what we call *process* are a host of methods and techniques; some are very clearly distinguished from each other, labeled and defined, while others are general concepts applied to presenting any idea or body of information. Process is always open to the actress's/actor's interpretation, even when the text seems fully scripted and accompanied by stage directions. Just as with theater, a curriculum and directions in no way ensure, in and of themselves, strict conformity to the goals for learning. Teachers are always capable of altering the process to suit themselves and their audience, although they usually adhere to the general philosophy and direction. Some may opt for a "radical" approach that changes society (they hope), while others opt for a "conservative" approach that supplies knowledge.

Each technique, each method, every aspect of process is based on traditions, personality, subject, and audience characteristics. The subject matter or curriculum is what will be termed *content* throughout this book, the "stuff" a teacher is attempting to communicate, impart, and conceptualize for the audience of students. Content may take many forms, from facts to reasons, from theories to values, from personal statements to analysis, all the way up to sophisticated evaluations and ethical decisions. How this material is communicated is the process of *delivery*, but the material itself is the content: informational, conceptual, or emotional. Process is part of every teaching role, in or out of a formal classroom setting. This can include business meetings, vocational training, driver education, and a discussion with Mom or Dad at home.

Oddly, in the world of teaching, a body of content can be communicated in infinite ways, some of which seem eminently suitable to the subject, some almost contrary to its spirit. For example, a favorite high-school social-studies topic, dropping the A-bomb on Hiroshima, has been presented in many strikingly different ways. The A-bomb lesson can range from informational text, foreign-policy analysis, or decision-making problems all the way to debate on strategy and emotional condemnations of war, racism, ethnocentrism, the United States, and President Truman. Students probably come away from each of these different lessons with totally contrasting moods and knowledge.

The content may play second fiddle to the methods employed, or vice versa, but balance is often very difficult to achieve. Content can be formed by a combination of words, images, and artifacts. However, the total package of choices, and the emotion or lack of emotion in the subject matter, will have a strong, perhaps crucial, impact on how an audience reads, views, and understands that material.

Furthermore, the words and images supplied by a designer, the curriculum maker, shape the way the material is presented and understood. In effect, the content is contributing to an overall mental map for those in both the teacher and student roles. How we accept this content, whether we question its formation and sources or accept it as it is, depends on own knowledge base, instructional philosophy, and, most important, our personal commitments and values.[9]

Thus, a teacher who doesn't know much about language instruction and has been prepared to teach reading in terms of "whole language" may not have a grasp on why some folks demand "phonics" instruction. The content almost doesn't matter, because the argument tends to focus on the way the material is presented, without much consciousness given to its composition or base. Once someone is drawn into the argument and seeks to understand the issues, the choice becomes a good deal more important and the knowledge base tends to be more balanced, eventually resulting in a choice.

Content and process encompass many forms of teacher practice, expressed as learning approaches and levels. This includes lower to higher levels of information, comprehension, application, analysis, synthesis, and judgment (Bloom's *Cognitive Taxonomy*, 1956). Content can promote or inhibit audience interest in participating, determining their level of engagement. Instructional goals may vary greatly, and call for acquiring knowledge as information, knowledge as skills and understanding, or knowledge as emotion and attitudes.

Just how content is conceptualized, as didactic, reflective, or affective, can have an enormous impact upon audience interest and involvement. Content, for example, may be oriented toward promoting information, which is usually not that involving. Material may also demand analytical or attitudinal goals, or some combination that research shows will produce much more involvement than factual material alone. By contrast, content can be delivered in such a fashion that learners are "radicalized" and changed forever.[10]

Content covers a wide range of subjects, formal or informal, such as mathematics, science, social studies, language, art, music, science fiction, health reports, or auto mechanics. Which content is most worth teaching in a particular subject, and how much should be presented at any one time to a particular audience, are key questions to consider for an instructor of any level and subject. How this material is best, most effectively, presented is an eternal question in developing a teacher role. A process, whether discovery, group discussion, individual research, formal lecture, or debate, raises key questions about which methods of instruction are most suitable in a particular situation, for a particular audience.

To sum up, a pivotal problem for the actress/actor/teacher role is selecting a process, a form of communication, that closely matches and supports a body of content for a given audience in a particular setting. Thus, we are back to thinking about "situative" cognition and the distribution of knowledge in choosing an effective and satisfying role to play.

Cognition and Emotion

The fifth element of our five-part dimensional model, cognition and emotion, encourages you to think about "internal" processes of instruction: thinking and feeling. You might call this dimension a combination of reasoning and attitudes in a teacher's mind. This is a mental map of what knowledge, skills, ideas, and beliefs are important to your role development. Many conceptions of teaching seem almost totally concerned with knowledge delivery and knowledge output, but avoid values. The goal is teaching and learning information in mathematics, science, history, art, literature, language, and the like.

However, cognition should also refer to instruction that includes a scale of performance from low and middle to high levels of information

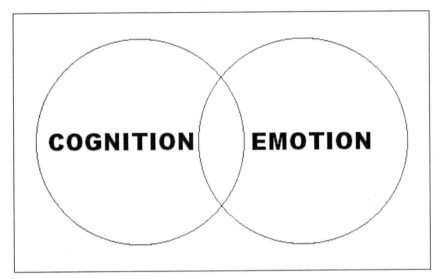

Figure 1.6. Cognition and Emotion

processing. Reasoning can range from factual recall through application and analysis to synthesis and evaluation.

Cognition in teaching is the sense of "knowing what," "knowing how," and "knowing why." There is a full range of human thinking and logic that is involved, using and interpreting information and ideas.

By contrast, emotion will encompass the range of feeling (Krathwohl, Bloom, and Masia, *Taxonomy*, 1964), from an awareness of likes and dislikes, through well-formulated opinions and views, to sophisticated expressions of personal philosophies for life. Emotions and ethics provide the "charge," protons of feeling added to electrons of data. While cognition can be presented in a neutral manner, emotion demands feeling and judgment. A positive or negative affect is almost always associated with emotion that demands decision making, judgment, and taking a stand on a subject. While cognition is about understanding and applying content, emotion is about organizing feelings into defensible values and beliefs.

There are "taxonomies" for levels of cognition and for levels of affect, or emotion, developed by Krathwohl (1964) and other associates, that distinguish between categories for knowing and for feeling. These category sets, invented several decades ago, are so well honed that many teachers use them as guides to create tests and survey questions for students. Levels are also built into newly popular rubrics, which offer criteria for judging student work. A conception of teaching roles can use cognition and emotion as organizers to think about levels of instructional quality and impact.

Cognition is a "reflective intelligence" encompassing memory and reasoning skills, synthesis, and evaluative procedures and processes. Feelings are a form of "emotional intelligence" encompassing a range of values from simple likes and dislikes to deeply held values and ideological commitments. Often there are borderlands where feelings and attitudes, knowledge and generalizations meet to generate passionate thinking and deep concerns about both intellectual problems and those posed by daily life.

In short, the ideas of cognition and emotion are key elements in developing teacher roles. The borderland between the two sets involves feelings as much as knowledge. The interplay of cognition and emotion always generates affective relationships, feelings between actress/actor roles and audience roles, extending to views of citizenship and society (Dewey 1915). There cannot be instruction without some form of emotion, even if the teaching is done through a website, computer program, or electronic blackboard. Knowledge delivered by media, whether TV, film, book, record, or live teacher, generates opinions, attitudes, and judgments. Ideologies and philosophies almost always bleed through content no matter how deliberately teachers or online designers try to avoid this effect, providing a moral framework for action (Dewey 1911/1975).

The choice between conveying knowledge with emotion or neutrally is a pivotal decision for a teacher. We need to think about the advantages and disadvantages of expressing feelings in teaching, for both the lead-character actress/actor and the audience/chorus. Do we treat audiences as groups with "average" feelings, or as individuals with particular views and attitudes? Do we play Moses or Deborah to the Hebrew children, and orchestrate a chorus who sings what we tell them? Do teachers expect students to blindly follow orders, or do they encourage improvisation and participation? Do we view ourselves in teaching roles as actresses and actors who can generate interest, or mainly as purveyors of data? Can we balance the two, data and feelings, cognition and emotion, so each will work for us in building learning?

The point is that emotion has as important a place in the proposed model of teaching roles as cognition. Educational philosophy has long been concerned with guiding emotional and ethical development.[11] Emotion is a very powerful tool for motivating understanding and building interest in a subject, while knowledge is better remembered when valued (Augustine 1938). Although emotion is, perhaps, underrated in practice by teachers, it plays a key role in the central relationship between partners in the teaching-learning challenge. Emotion between teachers and students can create long-lasting memories of affection, or punishment, influencing attitudes toward knowledge over lifetimes.[12]

AUDIENCE PARTICIPATION

1. How important do you think science and art are in developing teaching roles?
2. Would one be more important than the other? Why or why not?
3. How important would content and process, cognition and emotion, or theory and practice be in a teaching role? Would one of the pairs be more important than the others? Why or why not? Maybe you think audience trumps all the rest in importance. Why?
4. Overall, which dimensions or factors do you think are MOST important in creating teacher roles, for yourself and others? Why might you favor content over process, or practice over theory—or do you think there must be a balance between all the factors?

CONCLUSION AND CODA

As a conclusion, intertwine all five sets or dimensions into a dynamic whole, using a metaphor of rings of atomic particles moving in toward, out from, and around a nucleus or center. As each set of ideas is discussed, apply them to typical lessons you have witnessed, or to mediated learning. Examine examples of theory and practice from literature, philosophy, real-life classrooms, families, business, sports teams, and more. Where applicable, a brief review of relevant research will be cited for key issues in building pedagogical roles.

In the following chapters, each dimension or role set will be discussed in greater detail, with examples from classrooms. Finally, as opportunity and whimsy allow, the reader will be offered metaphors for instruction drawn from many fields and walks of life, to compare with standard views of instruction. These metaphors should enrich and expand your conception of the complex process of communication and reaction between actors and audiences, authority and democracy, individuals and groups.

This book is dedicated to the notion that all of us, as teachers acting in many capacities during our daily routines of life, could benefit from an opportunity to reflect on the possibilities and potential for expanding our concept of instruction. We can perhaps change our goals and our strategies to the benefit of those we value as an audience, leading also to more personal satisfaction with recognizable results. Let's consider our own roles as teachers to our children, friends, families, partners, clients, leaders, and students, including thinking as students as well as teachers.

**AN INTERVIEW ABOUT YOUR THINKING SO FAR:
MANY ROLES FOR A TEACHER**

1. How many different roles can you think of for a teacher?
2. Are parents, coaches, business executives, and politicians also teachers?
3. Do you see teachers as mainly playing authoritative roles, or democratic roles?
4. What roles do you play as a teacher? What roles would you like to add? Why?
5. Which roles do you think are easiest to learn? Why? Which are most difficult to learn? Why?

NOTES

1. S. N. Kramer, *The Sumerians: Their History, Culture, and Character* (Chicago: University of Chicago Press, 1963), 238–39. Translated from school cuneiform tablets, circa 2500 BCE. Many aspects of school would seem to go back in time to the very beginnings of instruction!

2. Greeno (1997) suggests that the many claims about teaching must be carefully adapted to local situations, that one size does not fit all.

3. Cobb and Bowers (1999). This article is a good review of cognitive theory.

4. Putnam and Borko (1997). The chapter makes a case for teaching accomplishing higher-order goals, rather than simply communicating information.

5. Alexander et al. (2002). This article offers an interesting view on the metaphor of "sales" as a form of instruction, much like common everyday teaching. This reminds me of the famous dictum attributed to no less than John Dewey, when asked what was the deepest American value: His reply was, "Sell."

6. B. Jowett (trans.), Meno, in *The Dialogues of Plato* (1892), 27–32.

7. Gardner (1995). Gardner's "multiple intelligences" theory holds that all students have abilities unrealized in predominantly verbal classrooms. Controversial, yes, but it is an interesting conception of the potential areas teachers can develop.

8. Slavin (1995). This book gives a comprehensive overview of the now ubiquitous "group work," demonstrating roots that go way back.

9. Hirsch (1987). *Cultural Literacy: What Every American Needs to Know* details what we all really, really, really need to know.

10. Freire (1972). *Pedagogy of the Oppressed* presents a critical and radical set of goals for teachers who want to change the world, especially for underdogs, but also raises questions about what is effective teaching versus propaganda.

11. Rousseau (1979). *Emile* is a philosophical ideal of instruction, and so civilized!

12. Foucault (1995). Worth reading on many levels, *Discipline and Punish* offers a disturbing metaphor of school as prison, at least for some.

❷

Audience and Actor

Domination, in other words, is everywhere. Those who lead revolutions are as much masters as those who defend Church and King. Freedom comes from pushing out the "master within," whatever his claims. By disbelieving in his legitimacy, you drive him out; at least your mind is free.

—Richard Sennet, *Authority*[1]

In this chapter, we will develop the idea that all teaching involves a *relationship* between an actress/actor (teacher) and an audience (students; Skinner and Belmont 1993). Even if you play a scripted stage role, you are still aiming at eliciting a reaction from your audience. A relationship can be tacit, silent and unrecognized, appreciative or angry; or it can be open, public, and participatory. Above all, it is a relationship, a set of perceptions and feelings, actions and exchanges, linked through communication at many levels. Levels can range from the factual through analytical to judgmental.

Teaching is a complicated maneuver. There are always consequences and effects for a teacher, but these are not always discernible to the naked eye, certainly not right away. Some effects develop quickly and can be read through audience feedback. Other effects may grow slowly over a long period of time. Teaching is an organic relationship between people, not an industrial model of input and output, producing an easily measurable outcome.

Teaching as theater is a metaphor performed by players in the classroom daily drama. However, that action or performance may or may not connect with the intended audience to produce the learning expected. Furthermore, although it is rarer, an audience can also act in

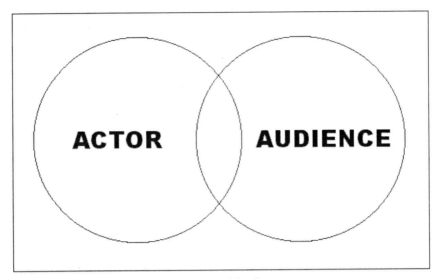

Figure 2.1.   The Intersection of Actor and Audience

the role of the teacher to promote a goal, whether they succeed or not. Sometimes, an audience can "rebel" in subtle or not-so-subtle ways that frustrate a teacher, provoking punishment, rejection, or reflection, or all of the above.

Teaching and learning are a lot more complicated than watching a "talking head" speaking to anonymous sponges! It takes real skill to keep an audience with you as an actress/actor, even when they are predisposed to look kindly upon your presentation (McCaslin and Good 1996).[2] And it takes still more skill to accomplish something, improving an audience's knowledge, thoughtfulness, skills, and attitudes in some way. Even more impressive is when a teacher can demonstrate a transfer of content and skills to the audience so they take charge of their own development!

COMMUNICATION BETWEEN PARTNERS: MONOLOGUE, DIALOGUE, AND "MULTILOGUE"

A central problem that lies at the very heart of teaching is whether to choose a role as an actress/actor or as an audience member—whether to act as authority or questioner, as communicator or acceptor, as driver or driven.[3] Authentic teaching, genuine teaching, effective teaching, in the view proposed, demands a two-way relationship between audience and actress/actor, whoever the role-players may be, a mutually respectful dialogue, with both sides contributing significantly to the exchange.

In the approach developed in this book, there can be no "deep" teaching without dialogue because the essence of instruction is communication, and communication requires a partner, one at the very minimum, to whom messages are being sent. (Even the self may be a partner provided you and yourself have a real conversation!) The partner can be a silent partner, a machine partner, or a video partner, but a teacher/actress/actor performs under the assumption that ideas or information or feelings or all of the above are being conveyed to a partner, and received in some fashion. Some partners are so highly motivated that they can extract great benefits from a teacher even if that teacher's style is rather plodding and unimaginative; other partners can barely sit still for a brilliant talk or discussion. Much depends on the experience of the partner and his or her perceived interests.

Here lies a great problem for most people who want to be teachers or regard themselves as teachers: The audience/partner must in some way respond by providing feedback, indications that the messages are getting through in a meaningful way (Meece, Blumenfeld, and Hoyle 1988). Otherwise, just what is the teacher doing except talking to her- or himself? How is the teacher an actress or actor on the stage of learning? Of course, many of us have known teachers—in fact, many teachers—who are communicating to audiences upon whom no demands are made for recognition or feedback, as the receivers are almost never heard from, and sometimes not even seen.

Favorite teachers who communicate "out there" are college professors who, as I do, mount a podium and provide a two- or three-hour lecture. At the finale they run out of time for questions, saying, "Oh, sorry, but time's up." These professors may be wonderful lecturers or poor ones, but in terms of building teaching partnerships they really are flying blind. They have little in the way of capability to ascertain their effects on an audience. They know virtually nothing about the impact of their carefully prepared words and research on those playing the roles of students, unless participants take the initiative to speak.

Applause, laughter now and then, and body language (such as sleeping) may be the only indications of feedback. Students may be furiously taking notes, hopefully on the main points, or daydreaming, snoozing, or staring at their computer screens; but if nary a question is posed on either side of the dialogue gap, nor any ideas exchanged, then we are all (as teachers) in the dark about what was learned, much less understood.

Teachers can also be thought of in metaphorical terms, as guides, coaches, trainers, salespersons, dictators, and so on (Ullrich 1985). Teaching, to use our theater metaphor, has much in common with acting on a stage or in a film, since the performer steps into a scene, plays a part, and seeks to express ideas for an audience.

There is a narrative flow over time, action, dialogue, sound, light, and influence. This is the reason we will refer to teachers as actresses/actors throughout this work. An acting performance can vary greatly in length, quality, mood, content, emotion, and purpose, but it almost always seeks to build a "successful" relationship, such that an audience feels different afterward, experiencing growth in information, ideas, or emotions. In different situations, the teacher/actor may have didactic, reflective, and/or affective goals for an audience. Whether the play is scripted or impromptu, the partners may judge each other according to set expectations and performance criteria, or invent them as they go along.

Key to teacher/actor communication are its structure and goals. There are relatively few modes of communication open to teachers, and these consist mostly of words, although images and, infrequently, objects may also play a part in the overall presentation. How these words, images, and objects are delivered to an audience is crucial to patterns of learning and building relationships. The choices are basically between monologue (one-way communication), dialogue (two-way communication), and what I will coin as "multilogue"—that is, some sort of multiple communication with groups (perhaps like "cooperative learning" or group work; Dillon 1988).

Monologues

A *monologue*, defined as speechifying by one, is usually delivered by the teacher to an audience. An audience could also theoretically lecture the teacher. For instance, during a revolution or rebellion, when the dominant authority is challenged and perhaps overthrown, it is the audience, the people, who tell the leaders what they should accomplish. But this is rare. Monologues are mostly about telling, storytelling, speechmaking, reporting, reading, and so on.

The whole point of monologue is to efficiently provide a body of knowledge to an audience who is assumed to be an interested and willing partner. But, as we have all experienced, this notion is often more of an ideal than a reality, as audiences may display an astounding lack of interest or attention in both the speaker and the material, and may misunderstand crucial points.

Particularly in schools where the audiences are largely captives, indifference or at best feigned interest often characterizes many well-intentioned teacher monologues. The best monologues perhaps are those of stage actors who dramatically present a playwright's ideas through their art and expressive skills.

Their audience is usually paying, and has chosen to be there, unlike many school audiences who must be present bodily, but not necessarily mentally. However, even paid thespians still have the problem of deciding if the audience is listening, really listening and enjoying the performance! Like teachers, they very much want to see an impact demonstrated.

And they like applause! When was the last time you were applauded in a classroom?

AUDIENCE PARTICIPATION

Write a monologue of your own that you are sure will provoke attention from your audience.

Dialogues

Dialogues imply that there is "real" communication being created between audience and actor, through both telling and asking from one to the other, as well as exchanging data, reasons, and views in the give and take of conversation. However, we all know that dialogues can be manipulated and channeled by a clever actor or audience member. It can really become a lot more like a monologue than a two-way conversation between equals.

Socrates, as reported by Plato, was a great master at this form of dialogue, in which he prodded, poked, and cornered his respondents into what was a "box canyon." No escape was possible except running out of the room or not listening. You just had to agree with the old philosopher or you would make yourself look like an idiot. Conversely, dialogues can be taken over by aggressive and knowledgeable students or groups of students, reducing the actor's/teacher's role to a minimum.

Dialogue may break out spontaneously in a classroom when a very emotional topic is under discussion. When very strong views are felt, student audience members simply are compelled to express their ideas with or without the encouragement and support of their instructor.

Actually, balanced dialogue between partners, a very desirable end indeed, is quite difficult to achieve for either a teacher or an audience. Someone (the de facto leader) is usually pressing the conversation. Others are trying to get into the fray, and these relationships may switch around often and haphazardly during a discussion or debate.

Thus, there is a sliding scale to dialogue, requiring us to investigate the quality and the quantity of the discourse between two parties who are assumed have the potential for an equal footing. How many fifty-fifty conversations have you witnessed between teachers and students?

AUDIENCE PARTICIPATION

Choose a few students and act out a Socratic dialogue together after a bit of rehearsal. Find out how the students feel about the experience: Do they see it as a real dialogue?

Multilogues

A "multilogue" (no, sorry, not in the dictionary, just made it up for this book) is more complex than a dialogue or a monologue. It involves many actors and many audiences trying to be heard at once. Players usually belong to a larger group that has been split up into smaller units for some greater teaching purpose. Furthermore, there may be role shifts during the conversation, with students giving information and leading, only to be replaced by teachers, and so on.

Within this multilogue there are many speakers alternatively taking on the roles of others, sometimes engaged in monologue, other times dialogue, with perhaps a third forming a somewhat anarchic shifting between and among many different speakers, with no one in particular dominating.

In multilogues, relationships build within the group rather than between individuals. Raucous town meetings sometimes seem to be multilogues, and these are fun for some, torture for others. After all, democratic procedures may entail lengthy discussion and debate. Now and then, a rebellion may develop, or an underground revolt, and this may affect politics and feelings in and out of the classroom.

Many people like order in a conversation—demand it and want to control it—but there are those who can comfortably tolerate a good deal of confusion and multiple speakers. In classrooms, there are activities and learning forms that specifically ask for teachers to promote multilogues, often in the form of panel discussions, simulation games, and cooperative-learning activities.

Students, the audience, are divided into minigroups of three, four, or more—whatever is useful and convenient to the material, say for a science experiment or a social-studies simulation game. Each group within the environment must work on a set of problems with each other before they merge again into the greater whole or interact with their teacher. Students may play teacher roles in their groups, or for the class as a whole, effectively replacing the teacher on occasion. Thus, multilogues allow for the development of many actors and mini-audiences to promote dialogue in small, face-to-face groups.

AUDIENCE PARTICIPATION

1. Do you like to deliver monologues?
2. How messy would you find a multilogue, or would you enjoy the free-form give-and-take of ideas and viewpoints?
3. Should the classroom be like a town-hall meeting? Why or why not?

Intersections of Teacher Performance and Audience Reaction

The multilogue is, in effect, an extension of the teacher dialogue, managed and constructed to promote interaction with a large number of actors, who are free to switch in and out of the audience role as they see fit. Here again, the rules of monologue and dialogue apply, since it is conceivable that a domineering individual or duet or triumvirate may control the flow and direction of a discussion. This speaker may, in effect, become the teacher for his or her group, for a time.

While monologue clearly gives one speaker the dominant role in a situation, and dialogue encourages two-way communication, multilogues promote a sense of participation by many, engaging a high percentage or proportion of the whole group, say 50 percent or more.

Monologue may be efficient as a communication device, but allows for little or no audience participation. This may inhibit or destroy interest levels for the teacher/actress/actor, as well as cause other problems for the audience. Rebellion or misbehavior in a bad situation may be the only way out for students who disbelieve or mistrust their leader and reject the messages being presented.

Dialogue promotes two-way interaction but is sometimes difficult to balance between actor and audience. A few are usually trying to dominate the conversation, but they may or may not be able to do so effectively. At least there is a chance in dialogues to achieve "freedom of mind" from two or more directions or viewpoints.

Multilogues go further than dialogues to stimulate the participation of many actors and audiences, within and among and between each other, but they are harder to handle in the sense of being more confusing and complex for the teacher and the audience.

Within the many groups and conversations, some jockey for power and position, and seek domination over others' minds. The subdivision into small groups, particularly if tasks are set and understood, gives quite a large percentage of the audience at least a chance to act and to think for themselves with immediate feedback from peers and colleagues. New leaders may develop as the conversation opens up.

Each form contributes in its own way to improving learning, but on a sliding scale of involvement, from authority at one end to democracy at the other. On occasion, democracy may seem like anarchy, and authority may seem like paralysis.

In all communications, there are always possibilities for monologue, dialogue, or multilogue. The direction of discussion is shaped by subject matter, purpose, circumstances and the overall atmosphere or context.

A great deal depends on the underlying philosophy of the actress/actor, and the customs and expectations of the audience. This is especially the case if its members expect to be told what to do, or believe that they have an active role in making decisions. Basically, a leader and an audience must choose or adopt an "ethos" closer to either authority or democracy. It is very difficult to mix the two modes in a classroom—community meeting or town hall, on the one hand, and supreme authority or dictatorship, on the other. (Aren't they mutually incompatible?)

AUDIENCE PARTICIPATION

What sort of approach would you emphasize: monologue, dialogue, multilogue, or a bit of each? Can you explain why?

How important is it to proceed "democratically" or to exercise authority?

AUTHORITY AND DEMOCRACY

At the heart of all teaching is an underlying, deep commitment to either authority or democracy, or perhaps to both in delicate balance (if that is possible), depending on the nature of the audience and the subject. Most teachers/actresses/actors are torn between the need to "tell all" to the unknowing and the need to draw them into the conversation as preferably enthusiastic participating contributors. The essence of authority is determined by who is viewed as the "master," leader, or boss. It is also determined by which people are seen as, or see themselves as, the "followers" or "serfs" or team members.

A rather dramatic way of putting the choice is to choose between the values of authority or democracy. Control or freedom is deeply embedded in situations of teaching, government, and other fields, where expertise, funding, and power largely control the content and flow of information. Google is the all-powerful purveyor of knowledge to most of our students now, an authority in cyberspace.

Teaching has a quiet and deep respect for authority built into the way in which children are treated on almost all levels, which is justified by the need for an orderly and efficient learning process and solid classroom discipline (Sennett 1980). Well and good, but control and order may extend from the social, and good manners, to the intellectual and reasoning processes, all the way to belief, right and wrong, and ethical judgment.

Conversations where the two intertwined parties, actress/actor and audience, attempt deeply felt communication can run into problems. Particularly when the emotions come into play—as in the discussion quoted below from an eleventh-grade upstate New York social-studies class—the process may begin as a "democratic" free expression of opinion but result in a reassertion of authority when the answers don't seem very agreeable.

T: So, what do you guys think Truman should have done?

S1: He really was right. He was the president and . . .

T: You mean it was totally right? Totally?

S1: Well, yeah, they know more than we do?

T: You mean the government, do you? Is that it?

S1: Yeah, since you said it, yeah . . .

S2: People who make war on us don't deserve to be treated well, not at all . . . We did the right thing . . . See Iraq . . . We can't let them attack us without responding . . .

T: But the Japanese were already defeated, so why did the U.S. have to bomb Hiroshima and Nagasaki, with atom bombs? Why?

S2: Well, they did not really give up, they kept on fighting and we had to teach them a lesson.

T: What kind of lesson?

S3: Blast 'em, blast 'em, that's how you get peace.

S4: We are the greatest power on Earth, and that's why everyone should listen to us. We know best . . .

T: What kind of people are you? Bloodthirsty warriors?

S1: Look, this is my opinion, I thought you really meant to let me say my views.

T: I encourage everyone to tell their views, but you are all so one-sided. Isn't anyone here for a peaceful solution?

S3: Yeah, I like peace, but if you can't have it, then blast 'em!

S2: [In an aside to S4] I think this is the end of the conversation . . . T isn't happy with us 'cause we don't say what he wants us to say . . . uh?"

Conversation in a history classroom, Middle School, Queens, New York, on June 3, 2007.

Teaching peace is very worthwhile; but if it is imposed, rather than negotiated, then students will tend to cease communication, or revert to a formalistic, polite, but banal series of responses to questions. A dialogue or multilogue must be led by a teacher who is willing to listen to answers and opinions, even when these are conservative or liberal and work against his or her own views.

Once authority takes over a teacher's mind and persona in a classroom or other settings, then the curriculum, the planning, the instructional strategies, and nearly everything else flows from the actress/actor—the leader, the star player in the show. Sometimes, in modern parlance, this is termed a *teacher-centered classroom*, but it goes deeper than that.

It goes to a view of teacher as a paternal or maternal figure who has a firm grip on accurate knowledge, clear reasoning, and correct moral beliefs. It is this paragon's job to communicate to the young, to other adults, or to any audience in need of authoritative knowledge, direction, and judgment. This type of teacher might say, "I am right and you are wrong, right as right can be," and that's good, if accepted.

Most of us as teachers would not want to express our authority so strongly because we recognize fallibility. We see the need for keeping up with our field and other problems that may limit our presentation. Nevertheless, we *act* toward our audiences as though we *know the truth*. Teachers like to feel they are experts in some field of knowledge, and that is to the good, but this expertise may extend to a level and degree of surety that is simply not supported by the data. In addition, there are two major educational problems engendered by authority, and those are a tendency toward doubt on the part of the audience, and their tendency toward a lack of engagement.

The more strongly a teacher presents a viewpoint, and the more rigid a body of knowledge he or she presents, the greater the likelihood for disinterest and then disengagement by an audience. Just as we hope to have student-learning scores rise, and we have efficiently organized our instruction in an authoritative manner using a solid and well-reviewed, rather weighty textbook, students seem to lose interest. They perform poorly on tests, and provoke no questions or discussion in our classrooms (assuming we ask for dialogue at least!).

The "indifference" effect often stems from the assertion of authority, now often legislated through standards (Wise 1979). Authority is excellent for keeping order, delivering information, and controlling insurrection, but not very good at stimulating imagination or problem solving. As the actress/actor increasingly adopts the role of authority, acting as management, many students may become much more worried about behavior, grades, reviews, and tests. The real learning of the material we hold dear (e.g., mathematics, science, literature, art) evaporates. Authority helps us to "cover a lot of ground" efficiently and inexpensively, but perhaps not as effectively, or with as much appreciation generated, as we would like.

Thus enters democracy, the opposing pole, in which the actress/ actor/teacher takes it upon him- or herself to promote classroom dialogue and multilogue. These democratic teachers make students in an audience feel more a part of the action, providing them with a sense of efficacy and influence (Parker 1996). We move from a political atmosphere of monologue with royal tone and mood, where ideas flow from "above," to one in which all are citizens of the same republic, with a voice and a viewpoint to express, however limited.

In a democratic atmosphere, the teacher becomes the "Speaker of the House," rallying legislators to promote their bills, express their views, and vote on matters of common concern with other members.

There will be discussions, debates, dialogues, and panels meeting regularly to promote participation. The democratic enterprise of learning could conceivably go so far as to include decisions about the curriculum and content to be learned—perhaps even to the point of setting the agenda, formulating goals that are agreed to by the audience.

The audience itself (if they show initiative) can take over the functions of the actress/actor to a great extent (Ryan and Patrick 2001). They operate as an autonomous body responsible for fostering engagement and assessment of learning. Here we begin to have problems, depending upon the nature and makeup of the audience and its context.

In some places, students may really be able to manage their own learning to a great extent, becoming significant partners in a classroom, legislators in effect. However, there may be elements in the population that are inattentive even under optimal conditions. Some may be obstreperous or violent, revealing them to be class clowns or bullies, while a few may show skillful demagoguery, manipulating the masses for less than noble and educational purposes. Some are skillful in creating discipline problems or anarchic conditions for the leader.

Democracy has its problems, and authority, too has its problems. Somewhere in between the two philosophical poles, a balance can develop between the actress/actor and audience roles that keeps sufficient order to promote learning growth, along with sufficient participation to promote student engagement with the subject matter (Webb and Palincsar 1996). This is a delicate and uneasy balance. The educational and social system, though democratic, tends to favor authority over equal representation, control over imagination, and order over intellectual curiosity and questioning.

There is a tendency to view the actress/actor as an authority in both an intellectual and a moral and political sense. Texts and lectures are presented as true, to be believed and not challenged by the likes of novices.

Authorities like to be approached ritualistically with appropriate codes, approved social attitudes, and a little show of obedience. Democratic procedures and roles in a classroom, as in other walks of life, demand that the actress/actor in charge cede a portion of power to audiences. They have the right and responsibility to participate in decision making, even if this causes disruption and slows down accomplishments.

The whole point of engagement is to provide a sense of "ownership" of information, ideas, and beliefs to the audience. The audience must have room to negotiate and make decisions of their own, with a minimum of interference and domination by the leadership.

In the role of authority, a teacher simply tells the answers, provides a guide to ethical action, and explains just what the steps of good reasoning are all about. In the role of democratic citizen, a teacher asks audiences to question the accuracy of information and check conclusions, testing for internal or external reasonability, and provides a forum for alternative or multiple viewpoints to ethical decisions.

As you can see, these roles are rather at odds with each other, and it requires considerable juggling and adaptation to make both roles work in an educational setting for those who do not want to make a definite choice in favor of either authority or democracy. Authority is probably the easier role, which is why many teachers tend to like it: There is often a ready-made script and an established ritual or routine to follow, for example, "Pick up your pens, remain quiet, open to chapter 3, and answer the questions at the end . . . Note that the author indicates that the meaning of the story is . . . Recite the story . . ."

Democracy calls for a more flexible and open-minded view of conversation and questioning in an educational setting, more of a dialogue or multilogue. However, outcomes are not nearly as predictable, though participation levels should be higher. Audience feedback can be complimentary and critical in a "democratic" setting, and may even shape the direction of the exchange because the information, reasons, and views of each member are part of the whole.

Each idea contributed or initiated by the audience becomes part and parcel of the flow of conversation and contributes to final conclusions, even if these are only informational. The audience decides which are the significant bits of data to collect, develops conclusions, and decides (or consents to decisions about) which policies will hold sway. Discussion is the main form of interchange, and there are many methods available (Wilen 1990).

However, audience is also crucial in an "authoritative" setting—but for quite different reasons. The teacher as main actress/actor needs to assess the degree and depth of reaction to the communications delivered, in an effort to determine the strength and commitment of the audience to the ideas presented. Agreement, or at the least tacit acceptance, by an audience is necessary for a successful authoritative relationship to develop.

In both types of situations, an authority or a democracy, there are still actresses/actors working as leaders/teachers. Feedback is essential in shaping the next steps either will take, with the important difference being that the authority is moving in a predetermined direction. The democratic role-player is moving in a direction that is continuously negotiated with an audience, through sharing and argument (Kuhn 1991).

Thus, fundamental to the art and science of instruction is a settlement with yourself as to the type of "political" and social atmosphere you want to create in your classroom. Do you seek democracy, authority, or some mixture in between? This is a key decision because it will cast you in a role for many purposes: curriculum, methodology, ethical stances, and so on. You don't have to be "democratic" to be a successful or a great teacher, but the role must be clear.

Audiences are quite sensitive to mood and setting and soon sense the iron fist through the velvet glove. If such is the case, a rather messy social scene may result in which teachers and audiences cease to really communicate. Important issues go unattended. Some educational leaders claim to have "distributed decision making," sharing power. However, this experience may be more rhetoric than reality: The reality is one of either a distinctly controlling authority or a distinctly audience-embracing leader. Any teacher may occasionally fall from deeply held democratic principles and turn tyrant—particularly when provoked by misbehavior and indifference.

Therefore, teachers and students, *the decision for democratic, shared authority or controlling and directive authority must be made in any instructional relationship. This extends to many roles we play*: parent, teacher, coach, government official, representative, businessperson, or community-association head.

AUDIENCE PARTICIPATION

How would you choose to cast your role: guide, leader, dictator, director, panelist, or committee member? Why?

Do you think authority can be "distributed" to a few, many, or all in a teaching situation? Why or why not?

RELATIONSHIPS AND EXPECTATIONS

Audiences and actors develop relationships built upon both their expectations and common experiences.

As noted previously, teaching implies some kind of relationship to an audience, and all audiences have some expectations of anyone in the role of teacher. Unfortunately, in many situations, those playing a predominantly didactic, educational role seem most intent on delivery rather than either style (art) or content. Their purpose is to build up the intended audience's knowledge base, often with little or no consideration of quality or the origins and sources of the instructional material, whatever the subject or topic.

Instruction frequently operates in a setting in which the actress/actor holds the authority, or thinks she or he does, and the audience is seen mainly as novices, or receptors for the data being delivered. Feeding in knowledge and asking for recitation is one of the "bottom lines" for many teachers, an age-old tradition.[4]

Of course, as noted previously, without feedback or participation in the communication process, the actress/actor/teacher has little insight into the level, quality, and quantity of the audience's learning, or their emotional state. It is assumed, expected, that the audience is there to learn and the teacher to teach, but there are many problems and questions that can be raised regarding the nature of the audience-actor relationship. A major question concerns the type of expectations audiences have of their instructors.

Expectations have much to do with cultural forms about the norms and modes of presentation into which we have been socialized. Some settings, some positions in society, engender expectations of participation, like a town meeting, or a committee, or a panel. Other settings, such as theater, create an atmosphere for reception, for listening.

For example, a theater company provides us with entertainment that we volunteer for, pay for, and usually enthusiastically look forward to attending for our own enjoyment (and education). We have a set of expectations for this experience—often overlooking the message, moral, or instruction provided by the playwright and actors, who are, in effect, offering us subject matter with both a cognitive and emotional component, sometimes directly aimed at us, and at other times indirectly posed to us in the form of a fantasy or allegory.

We attend performances, shows, films, stage productions, and other art forms with little or no preformed relationship, but a link may develop over a series of plays as we get to know the actors and repertory. Further, we may grow fascinated with a particular company or playwright, becoming quite attached to the works of Shakespeare, or O'Neill, or Shaw, or Brecht, perhaps along with a particular actress or star.

As we attend increasing numbers of performances, we begin to sharpen our expectations and understandings of the content and the genre, the acting process and the style. Thus we build a relationship to our "showbiz" instructor, who is embedding messages in art. Of course, participation is voluntary, and we are not constrained or directed to accept either the content of the play or the manner of presentation as part of our assignment.

We can pick and choose among messages and styles, performances and adaptations, to our hearts' content. Thus, we "consent" to learn in our own way and be entertained at the same time, but the control of the outcome is up to us. We allow the author and players to set the goals and deliver the content, but we reserve the right of evaluation and satisfaction.

In classrooms, we often are faced with "captive" audiences who must attend school, and who may or may not be interested in the content. The reason for learning a subject is often unclear to individual students. As an audience, a group, they may not be volunteers at all, as with the theater, but "trapped" learners who are expected to meet a set of standards, pass tests, and reach goals imposed from somewhere outside their set of experiences. But students most certainly have clear views of teacher and subject (Stodolsky, Salk, and Glaessner 1991).

The learner audience is therefore a threatened species who must worry about their performances, as judged by the teacher in actress/actor role. This situation is portrayed as "good" for students in some ways, bolstering learning so they can live better, more successful lives, get great jobs, learn to adapt, etc., etc. Thus, the classroom is a "situation" often quite unlike either the theater or the town-hall meeting. Its members are not necessarily volunteers for learning (Brown, Collins, and Duguid 1989).

A teacher also faces a question of role definition. He or she is expected to lecture, give directions, ask questions, reward and criticize, share emotions, and present subject matter. But much depends upon the way in which these expectations develop through experience. Expectations are general, usually, and are derived from cultural norms, but the actual experience may change expectations for better or worse, depending on the quality and depth of relationship between audiences and actresses/actors.

Most situations, particularly in schools, foster a sense of passivity in student roles, since the actresses/actors are active, but the learners are mainly passive receptors, absorbing the valuable information being imparted to them. This is, of course, a very limited view of the range and possibilities for relationships, which can vary greatly but must usually be set by the teacher rather than the audience/students.

The reason for a teacher initiative rather than a student initiative in setting the atmosphere and direction for learning is that expectations in school and society are largely "top-down" (sorry, you advocates of democracy) and under the direction of a person or persons who are playing out the authoritative role.

To foster a more democratic spirit, authority figures (sort of an ironic contradiction here) must take it upon themselves to create a different kind of relationship, through direct experience, than was originally expected by the audience: a relationship that demands interaction, feedback, participation, and decision making. To borrow a simile from civics, the instructor who wishes a participatory relationship with an audience must create an atmosphere and a set of conditions in which students understand that they are expected to proceed along the metaphorical lines of a town-hall meeting in ancient Greece, rather than a speech by the head of a totalitarian regime, such as Mussolini.

Between these two poles, there are, of course, many other choices ranging from representative republic to council of elders to benign dictator. The point is that the teacher as actress/actor/leader is setting the stage, whether in theater, school, government, or business, for the audience to be much more or much less proactive, more or less contributory to discussions, and more or less a participant in decision-making procedures. Thus, forming relationships is a process of building another, a different, set of expectations into the link between audience and actress/actor. Once the process becomes established, an expected mode of exchange and communication, then a settled and comfortable routine will emerge for everyone.

Of course, there are always great subtleties in the relationship between teacher and students, actress/actor and audience, leader and followers, coach and players. People notice details that please or annoy them, gather ideas that stimulate or depress them, and make judgments that are positive or negative about the same performance, depending on their level of observation, activity, skills, and interests. People, younger or older or mixed audiences, particularly if passive, have a lot of time to observe the teacher in great detail, and can focus on the most amazingly little tics, tics that the teacher may have been completely unaware of, and has paid not the least bit of attention to.

Audiences are there to "record" the presentation as direct personal experiences, and their perceptions may be quite different from those intended or expected. These group or mass views may eventually shape and influence the entire relationship. Popular opinion may be so powerful that a teacher's success or failure, like that a political leader, is decided by the audience, though it did not seem it would be that way at the beginning (Barber 1984).

A film, for example, seeks the largest possible sales, yet the audience may not engage, and the film will be a failure in terms of sales and disappear from the market. This is feedback through consumer decision making, with the moviemakers flying blind (despite marketing surveys before) in terms of what caused the success or failure of the product. The film/actor did not build the hoped-for relationship that would have produced huge sales.

Yet the film may reappear on video and find a large rental market later on, under different social and political conditions. There is always hope in the relationship between audience and teacher, curriculum, and content.

There is always a relationship developing through experience, in every walk of life, between actress/actor and audiences. Classroom relationships may be among the closest and most interactive of all, other than the ties that bind parents and peers. In rare circumstances, members of an audience, or groups within the audience, may become highly engaged and excited, attempting to exert control over the relationship, to the point of playing or directing the teacher/actress role over the teacher.

This level of audience expression is fairly rare and not generally as valued as it should be, for fear of potential anarchy and rebellion. However, rebellion, strong feeling, and liveliness are symbols that the teacher/actor has touched upon an emotion, a care, an issue, or an idea that strongly affects an audience's deeply felt concerns.

After all, audience emotion or affect is a sign of interest. We would prefer it to be positive rather than hostile, seeking applause over tossed tomatoes, but at the very least negativity shows that interest is alive if not well. Engagement and expression are strong forms of feedback for an actress's/actor's/audience's set of expectations that are decidedly in favor of active leaders and passive "students."

AUDIENCE PARTICIPATION

Prepare two or three examples of teachers whom you view as promoting a "democratic classroom," alongside two or three promoting some form of "authoritative" classroom. What were the key similarities and differences?

PURPOSE AND PERFORMANCE

Each presentation by an actor has a purpose, or at least we hope it does. The audience arrives with a purpose, too, usually based on their expectation of what is going to happen. Expectations may vary with setting and function. A play in a theater, for example, is expected to be well acted and interesting, engaging the intellect and the emotions.

A civic meeting is expected to be democratic, with all in attendance being allowed a brief time to express and exchange their views, and with all present who hold the franchise having a final vote in deciding the outcome. A sports event, for example, is expected to be an exciting event, with each team exerting their utmost to win, and with the fans (the audience) demonstrating their active support for one side or the other.

A classroom, by comparison, is expected to provide instruction in a subject area in a way that improves the knowledge, understanding, and critical skills of the learners to the satisfaction of both parties along some sort of public measure of achievement, for individuals and for the group as a whole. Popularity is seldom an expected issue in a classroom, but audience likes and dislikes, the desire to win or succeed, still matter very much, just as for a sports team.

Thus, the purpose or function of an event, a performance, an act, shapes the audience's expectations profoundly. Engagement may or may not result from a performance, as there are no guarantees for the actress or actor, nor does an audience necessarily know how or why it will evaluate its experience based on its expectations. As a relationship is fluid and evolving, it might purposely or inadvertently affect one or more vital aspects of the teaching model. A performance such as a hands-on creation of a mathematical model in a classroom may cause a great deal of excitement but not necessarily result in much demonstrable, measurable learning achievement on a conventional test of geometry.

Conversely, a performance in which each geometric theorem and application is laboriously described may be quite plodding and directive, yet demonstrate that the audience has understood the messages very well, and could achieve relatively high scores on a test, quiz, or essay. However, different measurement devices may show that the exciting performance did change affect significantly, causing more positive attitudes toward mathematics, while the plodding performance did not produce much, if anything, in the way of feelings. Students might decide that they loved math after the first lesson, but found the subject boring after the second.

These examples provide illustrations of a quandary in the audience/leader-teacher/student relationship, which is frequently pulled apart by tensions between purpose and performance. Results may occur that were not intended, and unexpected attitudes may destroy hoped-for results. Simply to set a goal is a necessary but *not* sufficient guarantee that a performance will carry through in such a way that the audience achieves the objective.

A goal must be worthy and viewed positively for audience impact, awakening their interest, while a performance must express, adapt, and connect that goal with the audience's capabilities and background knowledge. Drama may greatly capture and enhance attention, but prove very difficult to measure with a conventional test.

Lecture may impart the basic ideas and knowledge of a subject, one that the teacher believes students must know to develop properly; but a teacher may judge that the results seem effective, only to learn later that growth has stalled due to negative views of the subject as a whole (and perhaps the teacher's methods as well)—so negative that students express boredom or hatred with respect to the discipline.

There may also be confusion between ideas of effectiveness and efficiency in the way actresses/actors and audience interact. It's time to consult research on effectiveness (Walberg 2000). Each side needs to find out what the other side thinks of as their purposes and their problems, and then proceed accordingly—which, of course, requires a considerable amount of feedback and connection between the parties in the relationship. An actress/actor may believe that the audience absorbed the information, the emotional messages, delivered to them because they did not fall asleep or rebel but took notes assiduously and asked polite questions of clarification.

The audience members, if polled as a group, might think that they were getting along, and going along, for the purposes of mastering a subject they wanted to conquer, but that the actress/actor/teacher and his or her methods were linear, didactic, and boring, while competently reflecting pupil expectations of the topic under study.

AUDIENCE PARTICIPATION

Gather in groups and choose several political leaders, sports coaches, or actresses/actors and compare them to teacher roles: Do they usually get their ideas across more by appeal to "democratic" means or "authority"?

A KEY ISSUE FOR ACTOR/ACTRESS-AUDIENCE RELATIONSHIPS

Here we come to a key issue for actresses/actors and audiences: the trade-off between effectiveness and efficiency. Building a relationship takes time and input, emotion as well as intellect, and may indeed stretch out the amount of time allotted to "cover" a certain topic or subject. Alas, when input is summarized, sped up, condensed, amassed, and packaged in large amounts, an audience finds itself less capable of *both* enjoying and understanding the content. As this perception and attitude develop, the relationship may decline and sour.

In the case of school classrooms, students may think that the teacher has gone well beyond their level of comprehension, and at a speed that inhibits their intellectual and emotional growth. Knowledge, as a quantity, may increase geometrically, demanding extensive use of memory skills, while comprehension can decline from information overload, resulting in a feeling of inadequacy. Students may then feel lack of self-confidence, a situation that promotes hostility toward the teacher. If allowed to continue over long periods, poor student attitudes lead to a job that most would like to leave.

Worse yet, teachers can become punitive and sarcastic toward an audience due to misbehavior and bad manners. A combination of declining scores, boredom, a lack of discussion, and poor essay writing produces an audience likely to disengage altogether. This group exhibits behavior patterns that require disciplining and extreme authority. Audience-actor relationships suffer, which makes the job exhausting and difficult for most teachers in the field.

In a relatively anarchic classroom, the teacher must reassert control, enforcing authority and diminishing democracy. This is a costly process in terms of learning, as it takes time away from both content and process. In much the same way, actresses/actors do not like to be booed or hissed from the audience; nor do most political leaders, high or low, enjoy heckling, protests, and disorderly feedback from their constituents.

Performers want to be rewarded for their efforts, but players often forget that the audience members are performers as well, even though only respondents. They deserve positive feedback from their leader to bolster and stimulate a sense of self-confidence—even perhaps when they are doing just a little better than they were before, which may have been quite poorly. Purpose and performance on both sides must intersect and result in mutual support for a positive, growing relationship.

UNDERSTANDING AND EMOTION

Communication, the hallmark of the audience-actress/actor relationship, can flow from the authority to the audience, or from the audience to the authority. In situations where the actor/teacher is playing the authority and there is mainly delivery of information to an audience, emotion may be limited. There are likely to be instances of humor, encouragement, exhortation, and compliments.

In democratic situations where there is a considerable give-and-take of ideas between actress/actor and audience, feelings and emotions may be extended to personal exchanges of experiences. Personal exchange gives a sense of belonging to many classrooms. Different views are accepted and legitimated, including storytelling, ethical positions, and playful teasing or commentary. Creativity will blossom and grow (Massialas and Zevin 1983).

The actress/actor and audience, particularly if they have been developing a shared experiential base, may be willing to pun, joke, satirize, and characterize each other's personal positions in a good-humored way. The lesson or performance as a whole takes on a "personal" cast, more like the town meeting in a small village than a huge rally. A classroom or social setting thus becomes much more like a closely connected community. A sense of "team" develops, often generating even more exchanges among participants.

A caring teacher, projecting warmth, is usually also able to engender a positive identification from audiences. Whether this is done through expressions of shared values, care and attention to learning development, strong sense of subject matter, or positive feedback, emotions are presented publicly as a way of building rapport with an audience.

No teacher, in any role, can escape the judgment of an audience. Much of that judgment rests on an emotional basis, not necessarily a cognitive basis. Alas, a brilliant but driven, cold and demanding teacher can be respected, but will be unlikely to be loved. And this lack of love or affection will probably diminish students' accomplishments in the long run, depending upon their motivational levels and the degree of support they need to succeed.

In any case, the point is that understanding and learning growth are inextricably tied up with the emotions of both actresses/actors and audiences. Increasing communication, especially positive and participatory communication, expands the teacher's democratic role. While authority may be more efficient in increasing knowledge and test scores, democratic leaders may be more effective in building affection and participation. Higher-quality communication including personal exchanges would logically enhance a teacher's image and create a stronger sense of community.

THE ROLE OF DIAGNOSIS AND JUDGMENT

A key problem for actors and audiences, teachers and students, is the need for continuous diagnosis and judgment. The actress/actor, as previously noted, needs positive feedback in the form of approval, affection, or applause. There is also a need for respect and a sense of fear or success from an audience.

Players in a show want to know how the audience feels about the play. Was their reaction approval or lack of interest? Would they come round again and buy another ticket? Otherwise, proceeding, moving on, is dangerously similar to flying in a fog. The teacher is never quite sure what is happening if feedback falls off and silence reigns. Will you suddenly get hit by a seagull or spitball? Or join a flock of geese and fly in V formation? Will the motor cut off, and your lesson fail? Will you parachute to safety? In short, reaction and feedback are essential to judging the state of an audience.

For the teacher, feedback is as necessary as for the students, but if interaction between audience and actor is not totally formal or suppressed, then through questions and inquiries, the instructor can discover what his or her audience thinks and feels and understands about a lesson, unit, topic, course, or program.

Of course, this does not necessarily mean that the students will freely provide their innermost feelings and judgments. Just as teachers may feign conformity to administrative rules, students may pretend they are docile and in agreement. They may be shy, afraid, or angry, or simply need more time to think about an assessment. They may simply not care, or they may be actively antagonistic.

Inner thoughts and true learning are hidden from view unless a teacher's questions are thoughtful and probing, and perceived as sincere and well-meaning. If the context and questions seem meaningful to the students, they may respond with insights into their experience, and this can guide the teacher's next moves and choice of materials, thereby enhancing the overall relationship with an audience.

There is no "serious" teaching without reciprocity and reflection, along with dialogue or feedback from both sides (Zeichner and Liston 1996). Dialogue must take a direction, a shape, a structure, and a form to go anywhere in terms of intellectual and moral growth.

Expressions may be verbal communication, discussion, or debate; written essays or test performances; or extended surveys or personal interviews.

Body language, pose, and facial expressions can also serve as a guide to what is happening in the relationship. Audience and actors/actresses are watching for clues as to how each is evaluating the performance of the other. The teacher in the role of actress/actor must make judgments based on these verbal, visual, and written clues. Participants in the drama decide how to move forward, how to assess individuals, which grades to assign. The metaphor of theater bears a close similarity to the classroom in testing effective communication.

The greater the quality and quantity of feedback, dialogue, and multilogue an actress/actor teacher has available from an audience, the more accurate will be the evolution of an overall performance. Reading cues expertly, a teacher shifts and adapts to those cues and clues from the audience. Varied feedback from a wide audience is much more reliable than random or selective inferences.

Continuous and consistent reciprocity from the teacher makes an audience feel that you are interested in their ideas and their development. You recognize their contributions to the enterprise of learning. By contrast, in a more "formal" context, it is less likely that students will reveal deeply perceived or felt evaluations of instruction or curriculum.

AUDIENCE PARTICIPATION

1. How much interaction do you hope to have with an audience?
2. What do you think is an optimal level of interaction?
3. How do you know when or if an audience is "with you" or "against you" as a teacher, and does that matter to you?
4. How formal or informal do you think a relationship should be to most effectively promote "learning"? How did you decide?

CONCLUSION AND CODA

Thus, a teacher has an opportunity for building, sustaining, and enhancing relationships with audiences, much like actors in a theater.

However, teachers can encourage a much greater degree of interaction than an actress or actor playing a role to a theater audience (Wise 1979).[5] The teacher can build a relationship with a student audience on a sustained basis. Relationships blossom or sour over a regular and relatively lengthy time period. Theater is usually a more sporadic experience, and probably less damaging.

A leader communicating views and content from "on high," or through TV or other media, must rely on polls, ratings, citizen letters, or news commentary for feedback. An actress/actor on a stage must seek audience feedback largely through formal applause (or boos), body and facial expressions, and occasional questions—and, of course, ticket sales. Neither has the sustained contact of a classroom.

Teachers have roles with a great deal more potential for building an insightful quality relationship with an audience than the role of either a political authority or a stage player provides. Students get to know their teachers very well as they are on stage nearly every day, and teachers get to know their audience too. As both learn to share ideas and emotions, the space between them diminishes. The two circles slowly move together with more overlapping.

The teacher playing the actress/actor role has the time and motivation to learn student character and capabilities. He or she gets to know a particular audience's problems and complaints, their grasp of the curriculum, in ways as deep and engaging as perhaps only parents and peers ever achieve.

**AN INTERVIEW ABOUT YOUR THINKING SO FAR:
AUDIENCE AND ACTOR**

1. How important is it to play the role of an actor or actress in a classroom?
2. Are acting roles exactly like teaching roles, and vice versa?
3. Do audiences like drama? Do audiences like authority? Do audiences prefer democracy?
4. Which teaching roles seem to really please audiences, and please people in general?
5. How would you choose a role for a particular audience?
6. What sort of overall philosophy would you select for your own personal teaching style? Why?

NOTES

1. Sennet (1980), 42.

2. Listening is one vitally important teacher ability, but good listeners in my opinion are rather rare. Most teachers seem obsessed with getting the subject across or making sure students understand directions.

3. Roby (1988). The chapter offers an interesting overview of the many openings for discussion across a wide array of subjects and situations.

4. Hoetker and Ahlbrand (1969). This overview is an important reminder of how difficult change is in the teaching profession.

5. Learning is highly individual, and many teachers who give their all to following the city, the state, the official curriculum, and all directives may never gain or lose the bond between audience and actor/actress.

3

Teaching as Art and as Science

Praise then
The arts of law and science as of life
The arts of sound and substance as of faith
Which claim us here
To take, as a building, as a fiction, takes us
Into another frame of space
Where we can ponder, celebrate, and reshape
Not only what we are, where we are from
But what in the risk and moment of our day
We may become.

—Josephine Miles, "Center"[1]

In this chapter, you are invited to imagine yourself playing two new roles in teaching, as art and as science. Metaphors for teachers as artists abound (Sarason 1999). For example, as artists, teachers are like stage players. As scientists, teachers are like managers of industry. Artist teachers foster creativity and discovery. Scientist teachers foster precision and production. Self-expression is a goal of the artist, while the application of principles and laws is a goal of the scientist. We can draw distinctions between teaching as an art and teaching as a science but also develop relationships between the two concepts (Skinner 1954). Dichotomies in education are largely false because teaching is a complex act of overlapping goals, theories, and practices.

But let us start with a few distinctions—but not dichotomies in opposition! Distinctions are usually framed in terms of differences, so definitions of art and science are different. However, art and science also intersect at many points. These intersections influence every aspect of teaching and learning because metaphors are merged

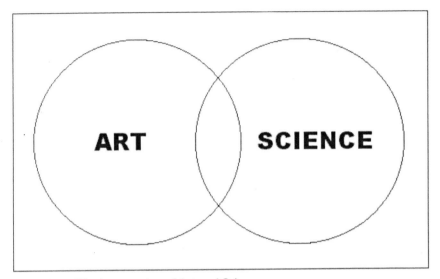

Figure 3.1.   The Intersection of Art and Science

rather than separated. For example, a teacher relates to and deals with people, building links with an audience. The persona projected may be classified as mainly art, based on a sense of emotional intelligence. However there are underlying psychological principles for engagement and intellectual development that guide a teacher. These principles may be viewed as mainly a science. How a teacher projects a "stage" persona, a "personality," to an audience should, for example, be seen largely as art, the projection of a dramatic presence. However, sociological studies may help the teacher relate to particular audiences, especially if the teacher has no experience with them. The theories of learning and pedagogy that guide a teacher's questions and responses to students can be classified as mainly science, drawn from research-based experimentation.

As part of the art of instruction, a teacher adapts to and takes advantage of different contexts and situations, based on a sense of people, attitudes, and feelings. Instructional principles that guide a teacher's choice of methods and materials are part of science, founded on many decades of research studies. How a teacher builds an overall atmosphere for creativity, for spontaneity, for imagination, is also an art. All of these skills and practices coalesce into a distinctive, personal style of teaching. The use of humor, choice of curriculum, manner of presentation, and stage presence are integrated into style. This is not just a matter of personality, as in "born a teacher," but a matter of integrating knowledge, skills, and experience into a stage presence.

Organizational forms and structures that guide a teacher's routines and assessments are likely to be predominantly scientific, with the outcomes expressed as measurements. Tests produce scores, but scores don't always tell us much about the reasons for student skills and growth. We also need the artful teacher to diagnose student strengths and weaknesses from daily classroom performance. Which stage personalities are formed, and how these are joined with research-based learning and teaching strategies, represents *the intersection of art and science*. The shared space results in a new and more dynamic place that is greater than the two separate dimensions. Fusion, rather than fission, dominates in our atom. The teacher who plays both the art and science roles is skillfully balancing and integrating two roles to stimulate audience learning.

DEFINING A ROLE FOR ART AND A ROLE FOR SCIENCE IN TEACHING

Art refers to all those matters of instruction that involve style and personality, the less tangible realities of teaching often overlooked in standard textbooks. These intangibles, however, can make or break the enterprise of relating actress/actor to audience. Acting as parent, leader, principal, or instructor, a teacher projects style and personality *in the role of actress/actor*. This stage persona may provoke great admiration and attention, indifference, or, worse yet, strong dislike. Audiences, whatever you may think, know what they like. That is a burden of teaching: You are tied to your audience.

A key force in artistic expression, a process of communication, is the attention and emotion art arouses. Affective as well as cognitive understanding, generated by a teacher, imbue an entire audience or group with an emotional view of teacher and subject (Eble 1988). This view can be positive or negative (but rarely neutral), inhibiting or encouraging learning. In artistic teaching, the medium—the emotional tone—of expression may be as important as the message delivered. In scientific teaching, the message, the content, tends to predominate, since the focus is usually on subject matter, which submerges but does not obliterate emotion and style of instruction. Science wants results, data, figures; art is happier with creativity, innovation, and style.

Style can be thought of as the manners and techniques used by a teacher to capture and keep audience attention. This includes expressions of empathy, inquiries about student feelings, favorite questions, group strategies, and self-reflections. There can be a good deal of variation in style since there are virtually infinite choices for rewarding, criticizing, questioning, lecturing, socializing, and sympathizing—all common teacher behaviors. Style is what renders YOU unique, the teaching personality, distinctive, more than you.

Do you like to begin each day with a story or a news account, or get right into the lesson, with no fooling around? Are you given to drama, or do you like to keep deliveries low-key? Do you methodically proceed from lower to higher levels of questioning, or do you like to experiment by jumping between levels? Choices for each of these behaviors will become part of your style in the eyes of audiences, once they are familiar with your approach.

Personality may be a teacher's projection of her or his persona on the stage of education, and not necessarily the hidden, "true and authentic" dressing-room personality. The two personae may be closely related or quite different. Much of a teacher's personality, as perceived by audiences, involves emotions: attitudes, feelings, and values. A teacher, in this view, is above all acting out a role on a stage. The teacher is projecting warmth and acceptance, frenzied accomplishment, and easy-going reflection in locations that vary with the audience.

The teacher is sending messages, perhaps using experimental methods (science?) or perhaps in dramatic and personal ways (art?). Both attempt to reach and influence a set of individuals in the role of students. As an audience, we can only assess what we observe, reacting to the outward manifestation of a teacher's behavior. A teacher's mastery of pedagogic and stylistic principles, exhibited in public, allows us to infer the level and quality of his or her "art" or "science," and the relationship between the two dimensions.

Let us look at art as the sum total of the ways a teacher projects a personal style and senses audience values and emotions. This includes both qualities and quantities of a style: strategies typically used to reward and punish, to explore and recognize audience members. Style forms into asking dull or stimulating questions, into creating a warm, cold, or neutral atmosphere for education. The sum total of art and science is a projection, both calculated and unintended. The sum total as experienced by an audience tends to be as much emotional as cognitive. They are either attracted to or repelled from "learning and teaching," or a bit of both simultaneously.

Every teacher, each one of us, projects a mood, color, tone, and attitude to audiences. This tone is sent to individuals and the group, producing an overall atmosphere, or teaching situation. The art of a teacher consists mainly in the way methods and content, theory and practice, are tailored for maximum impact. Artistic teaching tends to occur when an actress/actor is sensitive to an audience, moving them forward on a subject so they and the teacher both believe positive change has occurred (Leinhardt 1990). The audience, those in student roles, know more, understand more deeply, become more and more able to demonstrate a skill and knowledge they did not possess before. They construct an explanation that allows verbalization of the degree and quality of change they see as deriving from the teacher. In effect, they are evaluating the teacher as an artist and a scientist.

Artistic teachers know and can "read" students, as both individuals and members of a group. They notice cues and handle feedback so skillfully that the audience is impelled to move forward. Their desire and demand for learning increases exponentially. The audience may not even know why they are becoming excited and engaged by a topic they have never found very interesting before. Ah, that is art, the theater at work! How does a teacher become an artist? By really listening to and working with the audience, and by becoming a scientist who understands and can apply philosophy, psychology, and a theory to the learning situation.

Artistic teaching probably cannot happen without a base in educational psychology, especially an understanding of human motivation. How to get audience attention and draw out participants is an art. Let's look at an example of an "artistic discussion."

ARTISTRY IN SOCIAL STUDIES

[T plays several 1960s songs for the class.]

T: So I take it you've never heard these songs before, right?

S1: Well, two sound familiar. But aren't these from a long time ago, the sixties?

T: What do you think?

S1: Yes, they're from before I was born.

T: But can't you understand the songs? How does the "The 'Fish' Cheer / I-Feel-Like-I'm-Fixin'-To-Die Rag" affect you?
Any feelings?

S2: I think this is a strong viewpoint, and is poking fun at war. I think the singer is trying to get us to think about our feelings toward war, the Vietnam War.

S1: Yeah, yeah, that's part of it. But I'm surprised by the nastiness of the song.

T: What do you mean by "nasty"?

S1: Anti-war, anti-government, and he makes it sound like a circus. It's funny and serious at the same time.

T: That's a wonderful way of saying it—very insightful—but you don't agree?

S3: This is one of the most disturbing pieces I've ever heard. It's shocking to be so against.
  This is our country and we have to support it!

T: Right or wrong?

S3: Yes, if you serve the country then you follow its goals, even if you disagree.

S4: Wait a minute, wait! How can you say that? Sometimes people have to protest, because the government has made a bad decision, like now, like Iraq. Why are we there? Why did that war start and still goes on and on and on . . . ?

S3: I'm patriotic and you're not.

T: Whoa! Are we saying you must support the government to be patriotic? Are you denying J.'s viewpoint? Let's focus on the issues. How would you resolve this?

S5: I don't think it can be resolved. These are two very different beliefs.

S6: I think we should agree to disagree. Both have a point and we have to choose.

T: I know each of you has a view of your own, so let's express these and see where we come out, and maybe we could listen to another song, too? Huh?

S7: Yes let's hear the whole set. You are really trying to stir us up, right?

S8: Let's decide who is against or for war.

S1: I'm confused: Where are we going with this discussion? Where do we want to go?

S3: I think we need to hear some patriotic songs too. So far, you've only played the Vietnam protest songs, and that was not a popular war.

T: Are you accusing me of stacking the deck?

S8: More songs, more songs, and let's write one of our own . . . too.

T: A great idea. How about working in groups to write a song that answers one I play for you . . . ? But let's also continue our discussion . . .

S4: How can we write a protest song about today? How did they write the ones we heard . . . ?

They really knew what they believed, but I have to think it over . . .

Excerpt from a New York City high-school law and social-studies classroom.[2]

Note that students feel free to express their ideas, make suggestions, and even propose activities. The teacher is of course guiding them, but there are no fixed conclusions.

The conversation as a whole has the feeling of discovery, as students begin to set songs in context and interpret their messages. Emotional reactions are common, and a student challenges the teacher's lesson plan as "stacked." The teacher, as actor, avoids criticism and encourages feedback. There is an easy give-and-take of ideas. Views are neither approved nor disapproved of as right or wrong by teacher, only by participants. Overall, the teacher's stage presence is to guide and question, not tell. The style is open-ended, and student initiative is welcomed and complimented.

As guide, the teacher promotes an exchange of views, and asks students to check for reasonability and quality. The audience is supported in their efforts to both interpret the songs and develop positions and interpretations. Production, in the form of contributions to the discussion, is open-ended, although the teacher's purposes imply a commitment to debating political issues as expressed in musical terms. In effect, the teacher has designed an artistic lesson with a built-in issue intended to promote conversation and debate. The actor is "predicting" considerable participation and many discoveries of issues, content, and perspective. Process and content are joined to promote learning.

THE INTERSECTION OF QUALITATIVE AND QUANTITATIVE

An artistic view of teaching favors qualitative assessment of student progress, while a scientific teacher would hope for quantitative assessment. This does not mean that qualitative methods cannot be scientific or that quantitative approaches would negate artistry. Rather, the artistic approach is more personal, open, and critical, while a scientific approach is more procedural, planned, and statistical. A science of teaching seeks prediction, measurable results, and preferably a quantifiable conclusion (Popper 1972).

For example, based on research, interactive book reading with children is known to produce many benefits, including better participation, greater comprehension, and vocabulary growth. This is a conclusion synthesized from many studies, meaning it usually works (Mol, Bus, and de Jong 2009). However, the teacher-artist may discern that a particular book used with the children is too difficult. Responses are few and far between, and the children don't seem to like it. The book was assessed at the third- or sixth-grade level, but it doesn't work for this urban audience of largely immigrant children. The teacher-artist, critically reviewing evolving dialogue, notes that these students don't grasp the slang in the book, or miss the point of the story. Thus, the artist teacher, familiar with this audience, may conclude that the science of interactive reading, while fine for most, needs to be adapted to the new situation.

A science is the teacher's use of psychological principles and knowledge about group dynamics and learning theory. Teaching is the result of "action" research and personal experience, combined with tested communication principles. Art joined closely to science then plays a part in the overall production of knowledge and the fostering of understanding. Scientific know-how means understanding the "cognitive revolution" in psychological theory, its guidelines and principles, which a teacher-artist can follow. From these principles, the teacher can, to some extent, decide how best and most effectively to reach an audience and meet their needs.

From theory and research, teachers/actresses/actors can determine strategies and projections that help to set the overall mood. They can decide which students are most likely in need of stimulation. Teachers can choose how and when key questions should be posed, and which criticisms and rewards will have the most beneficial impact. Finally, those playing teacher can decide how to judge the direction and quality of a lesson, unit, program, or course as it evolves and grows for learners.

Much of a teacher's science depends upon a combination of professional development and educational research, tested by personal experience. Within research as within art, there are controversies about instructional issues and interpretations of findings, often with confusing results. When research conclusions conflict with each other, most teachers fall back on familiar traditions.

Teachers combine art with science, personal style and personality with educational psychology and social theory, to build an overall classroom atmosphere. Teachers seek to maximize the audience's opportunity to learn, to interact, and to get excited. The audience is, in effect, warmed up and won over by a teacher who skillfully makes use of psychological principles. A great teacher employs behavioral tools to build a system of empathy, recognition, and use of student ideas. Such teachers employ more rewards than punishments to promote stimulation of responses and interactive participation. Scientific findings therefore inform the art, and art is infused by a teacher's personal stylistic choices and attitudes.

A teacher's art is perhaps not as easily defined or judged as a teacher's science. Usually, measuring the impact of scientific teaching is more pointed, and draws upon clearer sources (Dewey 1929). But artistry is quite open to observation as well and may be judged as performance, like a drama.[3]

Goals and philosophical ideas inform the development of a teacher's art in a qualitative way. Curriculum knowledge and learning outcomes inform a teacher's science in a quantifiable way. Content and skills are subject to evaluation as both art and science through dialogue, tests, essays, reports, surveys, projects, and portfolios. Multiple-choice questions are measured precisely because they have been "scientifically" designed with built-in answers. By contrast, essays, even when assessed by rubrics, are very much subject to artistic interpretation. A well-written essay with rich vocabulary is likely to get a good grade even where content is thin.

Student work can be based on agreed-upon rubrics, criteria, and standards. However, quantity alone, without quality, only tells teachers what the audience memorized. Scientific measurement without qualitative standards will not do much to build a holistic picture of learning growth. Instructional goals join and intersect with theory, methods with materials, and products with outcomes, to express the art and science of teaching (Berliner and Casanova 1993). Quantity and quality measures together contribute to an overall conception of teaching, and a distinctive classroom atmosphere.

THE ROLE OF ART IN TEACHING

Artistry in teaching is a combination of personality and skills that add up to a style. The point of style is to project a stage presence that functions to create a classroom atmosphere for play and experimentation.

Outcomes are flexible and open rather than goal oriented and predict-able. Audience and actress/actor develop and cement their relationship through the teacher's projected persona. Rules are set, but the game's outcome is not fixed. Each player is encouraged to contribute to the game while the teacher learns how to relate to individuals and to the group as a whole.

Style

Each of us has a teaching style, even those who see themselves as faithfully following school routines. What gives each of us style is a combination of a "calculated" role and an invented role, which aims to draw in an audience.[4] This role is the actual or tailored upwelling of our personal preferences, prejudices, and preconceptions about teaching.

A scripted role-play, like a theater act, is probably easier to control than our personal choice of style. Following a model, with guidelines telling us how and when to be funny, what to say, and how to per-form, is easier than personal invention. We know when to present the monologue, provide a low-key narrative, or join a witty team en-semble. However, we are not really artists yet who have evolved our own personal styles.

Personal style preferences may be viewed as the expression of *selections* from our repertory of behaviors (the real you plus your sci-ence). Selections include choices for humor, reward, criticism, reas-surance, sympathy, horror, encouragement, and materials. Choosing a personal style means constructing a "stage" personality for others that aids communication and promotes learning. This persona is a mix of our actual self and our stage persona, a calculated role at first. With practice, however, this role becomes quite natural.

Audiences have to be comfortable with your persona as teacher, or your role will probably be questioned. We need learners to see us as teacher, as actress/actor, as boss, as coach, and as leader. For example, we may be basically critical in nature and demanding of achievement. We may be sarcastic or satirical—not always good "teacherly" qualities. We can suppress these harsh qualities in some situations. The "real us" will have trouble projecting the warm and fuzzy approach that is needed.

Our style, therefore, is a compromise between what we are really like and our stage persona, that is, what is needed by an audience to promote learning. The more a persona, selection, and calculation are consciously decided upon, the greater the potential artistry. This is because we have provided ourselves with a rationale and style for communication. We have shaped messages and techniques to meet audience wants and needs. We become experts in effective approaches to different situations and skill levels.

However, there is a problem, because an audience often represents a mix of abilities and skills. Audiences may need to know mathematical principles, but they may have low self-esteem. They see themselves as having difficulty learning the commutative principle. The teacher may see the commutative principle in algebra as quite simple to learn, presenting it matter-of-factly in a monologue we could call a lecture, with problems solved on the blackboard or computer.

But the audience may not appreciate this teaching style because they need emotional and psychological support to convince them that they are capable learners of mathematics. They are unprepared to take advantage of the lecture as planned and delivered. As actresses/actors, this group needs a warmer persona for math, one that projects a mix of empathy, encouragement, and dynamism. Students need to actively present and solve problems to illustrate the commutative principle. A teacher might make progress with jokes about "commuting" to work, or telling stories about how much trouble he or she had with the commutative idea. A good dose of empathy may relax students and improve their disposition to learn.

Choosing the role is an attempt to be more of an actress/actor upon a stage, with varying goals: entertainment, empathy, education, ethical challenge, or esteem building. This "calculated" behavior is planned and scripted with a particular agenda in mind for an audience. In some ways, it is more scripted and planned than the selected expressions of our persona, perhaps allowing less flexibility. A teacher-artist must meet the audience where they live, not where they want the audience to be as an ideal.

For example, let's say we have finished analyzing this month's novel, *The Return of the Native* by Thomas Hardy. The teacher has run it into the ground. Alas, no one in class likes it, but we expect our charges to have learned "to appreciate" literature. We already have an artistic problem in that few, if any, appreciate what we want them to like. This is not to say the novel or the music is "bad," but that our art, our communication to a specific audience, is not going very well. Our art is insufficient to produce the results we had anticipated. We have met a level of audience resistance that demands a new artistic approach. Thus, we need to rethink our style of presentation, the content, and the nature of our audience.

Our style might be changed to a more dramatic mode, flavored with student readings and dramatizations from the text. We might perform a role-play around the story, highlighting those dialogues and scenes we viewed as important. A review of vocabulary might be in order, asking students to adopt a new word as their own for today. We could combine wordplay with feedback from our audience, which we use to read their level of understanding.

Maybe we should play the author, talking with the audience about meaning and message in the book? Maybe we should show a film based on the book? And yet these approaches, too, might fail to "sell." The teacher perhaps should choose a new book for next "season" with this audience. On the other hand, if our acting went over well, we might now see higher levels of interest for a book viewed as difficult and dour.

Next time, the teacher will refuse to assign that Stephen King novel that was requested, because it is not "great literature"—putting new pressure on our sense of art. Maybe for dramatic effect, we should read a story like *Horton Hears a Who* to a highschool class in civics. Then the teacher can judge if the audience "gets it" on both a cognitive and a metaphorical level. Once again, a bit of science intersects with the evolution of style.

Persona

Part of art is developing a *persona*: a construction of behaviors, phrases, demands, directions, questions, jokes, and characteristics that are distinctively "us" as teachers. However, this persona is not really the same as our personality. Rather, it is how we want to look to our audience. Persona marries style to create a stage show aimed at engaging the audience.

Rules, values, and concerns are the keys to persona, which is designed to promote different types of learning goals (Wilson 1992). For example, a teacher may place great value on student-initiated ideas. These are ideas presented by students of their own volition during discussions. Encouraging student thinking is central to teacher-artist personae. Teacher-artists allow students to jump in and out of discussions without being called upon formally, especially during heated exchanges of views. A little anarchy stimulates imagination.

Some teachers might feel very uncomfortable about allowing students to call out answers or questions, preferring greater control and more formality. However, free-flowing discussion is inhibited by too much management and by too much direction. Therefore, we are willing to tolerate some confusion, some noise, and multiple interchanges to achieve a goal of maximizing student participation and the initiation of ideas.

Process may also be part of persona. For example, a teacher may regularly encourage students to take part in problem-solving activities. The teacher gently or forcefully refuses to give answers to questions that students can solve on their own. Student inquiry would be supported by content handed out to help them work out problems. Materials with built-in issues, problems, or questions, designed to evoke responses, engage students in the learning process. Some teachers choose this type of content to take advantage of its inherent motivating qualities, basing their decision on theory and research.

A teacher might adopt a style where solutions must be won through students working to discover answers. The teacher as artist would tell students the rationale behind this method. Empathy for the audience would be expressed, to demonstrate that they are viewed as intelligent thinkers. They can learn how to cooperate in working out problems with each other. This approach builds self-esteem, as well as promoting student inquiry. The phrases and ideas provided by the teacher would become part of his or her persona and style—examples being such sayings as "Let's learn to think for ourselves"; "You can do it, you can solve the puzzle—just look for the clues"; and "I have to work at this too, with all of you, because I don't know the answer myself."

Many writers discuss the "intangibles" of style and the mystery of the teacher's personality, but for the students, most teachers are very predictable creatures (Cuban 1996). Many do the same thing in the same way every day. In some cases students are encouraged to follow THE ONE RIGHT APPROACH day in and day out.

Worse yet, in many schools, the authorities demand uniformity to a common plan and curriculum, a "one size fits all" approach. Over the past several decades, there have been waves of "reform" with top-down pressures for conformity, usually to one model of teaching. Cooperative learning, the workshop model, the developmental lesson, and many other models have been imposed upon large numbers of teachers. Teachers conform to, adapt to, or rebel against this situation; mostly they go along, while sabotaging the process.

Audiences get to know preferences, favorite expressions, assignments, jokes, values, likes and dislikes, and methods. Oddly enough, this is where personal style plays a provocative and protective role in teaching, by giving us routines that we can also change. Unlike actresses/actors in a drama, teachers are not usually required (we hope) to follow a set script. Teachers are allowed to project a set of emotions suited to the character chosen for the play. To achieve the desired effects, teachers can alter script, plan, materials, mood, and strategy to fit the situation and the curriculum.

A persona, a distinctive style, provides students with a set of expectations and a sense of stability; but a teacher always has the element of surprise available. Teachers can (and should) unexpectedly shift tactics to enhance attention and surprise an audience with something new. A shift in emotional displays, such as sudden sadness or anger, humor or tragedy, is a way of engaging student attention and reinvigorating a lesson. Shifting or adapting a persona may offer greater flexibility than a calculated role-play that follows a strict scripted model. A model loses some of its power as an audience grows familiar with it and can too easily predict goals and outcomes after a while (although a new model can be selected).

Thus, a persona can evolve, changing as conditions demand, growing more sensitive to audience proclivities and interests with increasing knowledge and bonding. What students, audiences, see as the special "you" or "self" is what they see as your teacher persona. Style and persona can be cultivated consciously or may just evolve subconsciously, but they always have a more profound impact upon audiences than we give them credit for as we think about the seemingly more important factors like content and process. Over a period of years, teaching becomes a "method," much like coaches have favorite plays or actresses/actors favorite roles.

CREATIVITY

In addition to developing a stage persona and a style, artistic teachers try to be creative. *Creativity* in teaching may be defined as generating audience participation in making or doing something new to them, using their imaginations (Eisner 1994). However, learners need not simply repeat past efforts. They are encouraged to take "leaps of mind" into new subjects. Audiences must take action to experience the creative impulse. There has to be active play with ideas and materials for creativity to take hold. Unlike a science where we can predict (we hope) the outcomes, artistry/creativity is unpredictable and uneven.

Audiences are given the opportunity to be producers rather than consumers. This is a risk in the eyes of many teachers, because they are never sure about the outcome. In a planned, scientific approach, goals are precise and outcomes controlled, but there is not much imagination demanded.

In a creative setting, students have the chance to "do their own thing" according to a set of guidelines. The more open the guidelines, the greater the potential for creativity—but also loss of direction. If students are members of a classroom audience that is used to taking creative leaps, then clearly they will have greater tolerance for ambiguity. If the use of imagination is unfamiliar, then there will be less tolerance. A creative role demands tolerance for competing ideas and puts a premium on authenticity. Students, role-players in the activity, are asked to express themselves, not to repeat, mimic, or reproduce content and process. To respond in kind to teacher initiative, students invent a product or idea of their own.

And the teacher must react kindly, with praise and support, even when products and ideas are not altogether clear or logical. Copying or downloading websites is the very opposite of creativity. Imagination springs out of the minds and souls of learners.

Since creative teaching is rather rare, many audiences will disbelieve the stated goals. Or they may be so unused to creative endeavors that they are bewildered and confused by the demands. So creative artistry takes some getting used to by most audiences. However, if practiced regularly, creative surges often lead to feelings of strong personal accomplishment. After all, the products or ideas are owned by students and are truly their work, not reproductions.

Originality and imagination (even if modeled on known examples) are valued above all. To create a creative atmosphere in a classroom is quite difficult. Audiences must be convinced that their work is valued. They must be prevailed upon to use their imaginations! This means that the actor/actress-artist legitimizes and supports student expression, self-expression, in wide variety. Thus, a good deal of experimentation and revisionism has to be tolerated.

Teachers cannot demand "right" answers in a creative atmosphere. They must refrain from personal criticism of students. Whatever the product or idea, they must be accepting and professionally critical at the same time. This critical quality is directed at work, not at student personae, and should help the producer to revise and perfect the product. Students could be taught to play critical roles, working with peers to make suggestions and provide multiple points of view. Again, this takes attention on the part of the teacher, because criticism must be constructive to have the proper effect and fit the overall culture of creativity.

Of course, creativity cannot develop from lack of knowledge. Students must be familiar with the subject at hand and use models for action. Creativity may begin with products that are reproductive of originals. But the movement should be toward authentic expressions of student views and skills. The purposes or goals of creative teaching include assessment of the talents students possess, but to discover talent you must provide opportunities for expression.

If an artist teacher projects style, persona, and creativity, then students will be likely to open up and demonstrate the skills they possess. Teachers may be surprised that students they viewed as poor performers in some areas suddenly seem a great deal more attractive in other areas (Gardner 1993).

Reading and writing are much and rightly valued, but some students may have visual gifts, social gifts, and sports gifts that have gone unrecognized. Gardner's *Theory of Multiple Intelligences* suggests a wide range of abilities and "gifts" for human beings. Yet schools and classrooms tend to emphasize only a few of these, mostly linguistic and mathematical. This limits student potential and creativity.

Teachers can play the creative role in every subject and at every level of achievement. There is really no limit to creativity (we are not talking about genius!) if one is given the opportunity. Thus, the teacher's creative role is about providing opportunity. Designing a creative room includes setting up lessons, interesting questions, and hands-on activities promoting independent thinking. For example, in a second-grade class preparing for Thanksgiving, students are asked to create their own turkey pictures. No templates, please! For more creativity, let each student use different materials to create a turkey. You may discover some rather funny conceptions of turkeys, but these are authentic student work. This is what students can actually produce out of their own imaginations.

Rather than talk about the reasons for war in a global-history course, a creative teacher might play a role game of alliances. Students will come to understand why a group of fictitious nations fall in and out of alliances with each other. They will begin to see that power is a motive for expansion and dominance while having fun "being" those competing countries. Perhaps they will even evolve their own peculiar alliances without warfare at all, leading to new insights about how conflicts can be resolved.

A funny short story by Kurt Vonnegut can be closely interpreted and analyzed, which is certainly a valuable use of time. Then think about following the story with having students write funny stories about incidents in their own lives. And just to make this more challenging and creative, ask that the story be written in Vonnegut's style. Then ask that the story be rewritten in the student's own style—and if a student doesn't have one, ask him or her to invent it, please. It's an experiment: Let's see what happens.

Thus, a very artistic teacher is one who can adapt to many situations. This teacher can tell what an audience is like in a relatively brief period of time, and then move on to target interests and fascinations, being very much an artist in progress. This artist teacher can project ideas and stories, formulas and theories, setting a tone, mood, color, and texture. An atmosphere is developed that seems to suit audience interests. Artist teachers can project their goals and personae so well that students are almost effortlessly drawn into the subject. They begin to work, impelled by fascination as well as rewards and criticisms. Artfulness conveys a positive atmosphere of accomplishment, but with room for play and creativity.

This level of creativity is, of course, an ideal that is seldom attained by most teachers. Real life confronts us with conflicting interests, junior hoodlums, lack of materials, broken technology, and other distractions. Then there is the after-lunch crowd, the sleepy and the sluggish. But freeing imagination is an ideal to work toward. Through experimentation with the dual roles of art and science, a workable balance can be attained.

AUDIENCE PARTICIPATION

1. Would you like to add your own views on artistry and persona?
2. Would you develop your own definition of the "art" of teaching?
3. Is creativity a part of art in teaching? Why or why not?
4. Can you provide any examples of artist teachers you have experienced?
5. Do you aspire to artistry? Why or why not?

THE ROLE OF SCIENCE IN TEACHING

A science of teaching is about using precedents, research, and organized planning to predict future outcomes (Hiebert, Gallimore, and Stigler 1999). Generalizations drawn from both theory and practice, grounded in research findings, are applied to classroom performance. Rules or principles evolve from inquiries into best practice that can be broadly applied to teaching a subject, group, or situation.[5]

A science of teaching emphasizes systematic inquiry and testing, seeking quantification of results. Even observations are prearranged in categories or rubrics defining what the researchers/teachers will look for in student behavior. The metaphors of a science of teaching borrow heavily from industrial models. Student productivity is charted, measured, and summed up at the conclusion, converted into a quantity. So many units in biology passed equals course credit; so many courses in English equals graduation; the sum total means you are educated.

Of course, this overlooks quality and performance, the major concerns of an art of teaching. Not that a science is not interested in quality; rather, it tends to define criteria in narrow terms and judge success by output. Technology applied to a science of teaching enhances growth, speed, and efficiency. Student use of computers is now nearly universal, and schools, on the whole, are tightly organized. Yet we still live in an age of endless reform and dissatisfaction with educational performance. According to most measures, a high percentage of students are not up to standard on either basics or academic subjects.

But if we truly had a science of teaching, results should be much better. So we are moving to judge teachers by test scores, an easy way to calculate productivity. But this is a method that almost completely overlooks teaching as an art. To be fair, those advocates of a science of teaching, just like artists, want a quality result. They are only to blame insofar as they have provided the system with the tools for conformity and measurement of productivity, often mindlessly followed.

A factory model of schools demands organization and work. Therefore, planning, production, and assessment are required, particularly for mass audiences. Prediction of results should be assured by input. However, this is an unbalanced approach to teaching. Human beings, both teachers and students, are variable in abilities and interests. Even machine instruction over the Internet is the product of human designers of varying talents and philosophies. Each may or may not have a clear vision of goals or methods for teaching.

Teaching is multilinear, combining art and audience, science and actor/actress, in ways greater than any one approach or method. One side of a science seeks to establish principles, the laws of teaching and learning. Applying principles to classrooms, and drawing from established research, makes learning more predictable. The other side promotes the extension of knowledge to new ideas, inventions, and discoveries. To enforce a simple science of standardization is unlikely to result in quality ideas, much less discovery and invention. Both the creative and the applied sides of a science should cross-pollinate in order for deep insights to develop.

PRINCIPLES

Teaching rests on scientific principles that are research based, with important elements of practice. Practice is partially developed from the results of educational and social psychology, particularly the cognitive psychology of the past several decades (Demetriou, Mouyi, and Spanoudis 2010). From psychological and social-science research, we have learned a great deal about how the human mind works. This includes short- and long-term memory, formal and informal reasoning, and ethical decision making.[6]

While there are areas of controversy over the interpretation and implementation, fairly strong recommendations from research apply to everyday practice. Research covers every aspect of education. Studies focus on building memory, fostering thinking skills, encouraging creativity, improving group dynamics, and assessing school performance. Research also has something to say about building social settings and community influences on schools.

However, research tends to focus on selected student samples and tightly defined problems. Controls demand that most research focus on particular situations, although attempts are made for broader studies and inclusive generalizations. A "science" of teaching rests on interpretations of educational studies, rather than simply a reliance on traditions. Customs like writing notes on a blackboard, giving homework, or answering questions at the end of the chapter are also researched. Do we really know if each of those practices is effective? Generally, the answer is that the probabilities are on the positive side. Research may, however, yield other results for different audiences or under different conditions. Read provisos carefully.

Over a long time period, for a certain type of student audience, or on a particular school subject, researchers corroborate reliable and effective practices. If, as the actress/actor, you are using "multiple intelligence" findings properly, or if you have implemented a phonics program, it should work. Of course, you need to read disclaimers and conditions, and apply these to your situation.

Lecture is a traditional teaching method going back eons. Its effectiveness for certain audiences and age groups is supported by research. But in other conditions, lecture effects are greatly diminished compared to interactive practices. Students have many skills and talents that teachers may overlook. If teachers stress verbal and written work, how will they assess the impact of movement, visual thinking, music, or social networking?

There are always controversies over the meaning and interpretation of educational and psychological research. This does not change the view that a science of teacher action is research based.

Leaders of an educational community or government may set priorities for teachers based on a summary of research findings (accurately or inaccurately interpreted). They hand down directives for all to follow. But this is not exactly what we have in mind as a science of teaching. We prefer a model that the teachers interpret and apply from research-based ideas (Resnick 2010). Teachers adapt practices to audiences, from the very young to college graduates, from specific to continuous learning groups, across all subjects. Just as an artistic teacher must adapt style, research practices have to be suitable for a particular setting and group.

The adoption of scientific principles of teaching—for example, motivation studies—sets up a diagnostic framework for interpreting behavior. When a teacher, an actress/actor, applies and uses a research-based idea, he or she needs to adopt an experimental attitude as well, closely viewing audience behavior, examining results on tests and essays, and using other diagnostic devices to yield clues about performance.

Finally, in real life, teachers model practice from both tradition and research through a social system. Examples abound of areas where research has had a profound effect on daily teaching. For example, group work and cooperative learning have a solid base in community and research. Cooperative learning has a long and well-developed history, with many variants and results. From within these findings, teachers can choose from a range of strategies to vary and enliven classroom instruction, merging art and science.

A SCIENTIFIC DISCUSSION

Discussions can take many forms, from groups of two, three, four, or more to "jigsaws," a content puzzle put together by small groups into a whole picture. Along with fairly simple small-group tasks, there are complex and highly motivating approaches: role-play and dramatics, simulation games, and mock trials. Role-play mimics real-life events and gives students the opportunity to echo experience. Role-play and simulations have been studied and generally endorsed by most educational psychologists. Research supports simulations as adding a strong element of enjoyment and virtual reality to classrooms.

Despite informative research, however, many teachers do not take advantage of games: board, electronic, or kinesthetic. These actresses/actors seldom read from educational studies that might help them. Many rely more on long-established customs and traditions for guidance to daily practice. However, even the most traditional settings exhibit a mix of traditional, artistic, and scientific teaching.

For example, let's take a look at a recording of a seventh-grade geometry classroom in New York City and decide what elements we see as science based or as teacher artistry (Johnson and Johnson 2010).

T: Please form groups of four to work on our math construction project . . . [Hands out packets of materials to the class, one for each group.]

T: OK, now each group has a packet, and in it are assignments for constructing geometric shapes. You will have to build these and then think about their form and name from the clues provided. You can discuss the project with each other, but no personal conversations . . . OK?

Ss: [Work together on the projects . . .]

J: So, X, what do you think we should do?

X: Let's put it together . . . It's like a puzzle, so why don't we sort out all these pieces and have a look at how to put these together.

S: OK, I see about twenty-five pieces, and they seem confusing to me.

X: Well, let's move them around and see if they make any sense. Let's lay them out to find a pattern.

M: Patterns will help, if we find one. Geometry always has patterns for shapes.

J: I would rather talk about my boyfriend . . . He was really a pain yesterday.

S: Come on now, I want to get my work done, and you heard what the teacher said about personal stuff.

J: OK, OK, so let's move the pieces around . . . This is more fun than yesterday's homework, that's for sure.

X: That's the spirit. And you, S, what do you think it is?

S: I can't tell yet—too many pieces . . . This is a 3-D construction, right? So let's divide the pieces into sets of six or five and then see how they relate.

X: That's a very good idea. Why didn't I think of that? . . . [Work away.]

M: Hey, hey, I think the thing is put together this way, but I don't know what it is yet . . . It is very complicated and seems like a hexagon, or something. Maybe it has more sides than a hexagon—not sure.

X: I'm impressed you even know that word, *hexagon* . . .

[General laughter and multiple conversations.]

T: What's going on there? . . . Are you at work?

M: Yes, ma'am . . .

T: [Looking suspiciously at the group] Well? Any results?

S: We agreed to make sets of figures and decide how they fit together. That's our strategy, right, X?

X: Yes, and each of us has come up with the possibility that it's a hexagon or something like that, but we are not finished with our work. Maybe we will come up with a construction we can build but not name.

T: Well, that is a neat strategy, and an interesting comment. Maybe the other groups would like to hear about it? And who really invented it—you, X?

X: No, S gets the credit for the original idea.

S: Why, thanks.

M: Yes, but you get the credit for pushing us to solve the problem . . .

X: Thanks, M. And so let's get back to our problem . . .

Excerpt from a New York City mathematics classroom.[7]

As you can see in this example, the teacher has decided to conduct a "hands-on" geometry lesson with a group of seventh graders. The lesson is based on educational studies in mathematics suggesting that thinking about mathematical concepts benefits from constructions in groups (Ball 1992). Concrete action helps many pre-abstract thinkers. Hands-on activities derive from research showing a strong relationship between conceptual development and hands-on science and mathematics activities. Hands-on activities are proved more effective (usually) than paper-and-pencil geometric drawings or homework. Our exemplary teacher decided on groups of four probably because that is a "square": just the right amount of face-to-face participation for solving puzzles.

Content is supplied in the form of a packet of "parts." The students have to connect the parts into a whole, which is followed by discussion. Task orientation is enforced, making students stick to the task. However, one student openly admits a need to talk about personal matters during the math lesson. This student is probably discouraged from goofing off by the group leader. From the quality and tone of comments, X seems very work oriented; X pushes or cajoles the other three into solving the puzzle.

Nevertheless, probably the most creative comments come unexpectedly from S, probably not the best student and most praised by the teacher. The teacher, interestingly, directs control and inquiry comments to X, who is a strong group leader. X actually has matters well in hand, with the laughter in the group being work related rather than a cause for disciplinary action. We could argue that the teacher is needlessly worried about working toward the goal of learning geometry. She assumes a traditional role to foster better discipline although this may not be necessary. Art is used in offering praise and humor, encouragement for student work. However, no great outpouring of emotion or dramatics accompanies the math lesson.

It could have developed as a hands-on project from dramatic presentations. The teacher's "science" is better developed in designing content and implementing group work than the teacher's art was in interpreting students' attitudes and answers. Cooperative-learning theory, while well developed, is not always easy to manage with large groups assigned to varied tasks. A good deal of teacher energy and skill, art and science, is needed to direct a successful cooperative or group project. Interaction can move so fast that a lesson takes on a life of its own like a "swiftly moving river" (Lewis and Tsuchida 1997).

To sum up, group work can be very productive, but it is often difficult to "read" five or six groups working simultaneously. This requires a good deal of observation and moving around. There are occasional interventions, calculated to promote solutions, by the teacher, who may erroneously focus on control issues when students are having fun while working.

MEASUREMENT

A scientific model of teaching seeks to measure the results of instruction by the amount and quality of learning (Sternberg and Grigorenko 2000). How learning is defined is of great importance: This will loop back to shape goals and instructional techniques. Overall, measurement provides numbers as scores that attest to student performance in terms of overall skills and for specific subjects.

Mass education demands systems of measurement because so many people are being socialized into a culture that values productivity. We need to quickly and easily assess content and skills. Therefore, tests have evolved into standardized measurement tools that yield reliable assessments of knowledge and growth. At least, the results are statistically reliable, assuming an honest assessment.

The idea of measurement grew out of late nineteenth-century and early twentieth-century psychology that sought to provide facts and figures for knowledge and attitudinal growth. Over many decades, measurements have been refined and field tested. As educational systems have grown to include the entire population, testing and measurement has become a large and powerful business.

Nearly every walk of life now employs testing and/or polling in some form. From marketing surveys to tests of critical (and, less frequently, creative) thinking, people are constantly engaged in test taking. Results are often calculated promptly and easily, and scores eagerly anticipated (well, not always). Testing is now a science itself, particularly in education, where there is not a child left over the age of eight who is unfamiliar with the process of examination.

While a science of teaching does not necessarily demand testing, the ease and utility of modern examinations make them just too good to pass up. Formal testing has been part of classroom life for a long time, a hundred years or more. Quizzes, finals, midterms, surveys, and diagnostic reports form the language of school testing. Teachers need assessments as measures of both input and performance. In effect, tests are a form of audience feedback, and a very valuable one.

However, there is a great deal of confusion over what results signify, and how results were achieved. The industrial or factory model of education is pretty much satisfied with an output up to or above standards. The factory is not particularly interested in reasons, unless there are too many defects or poor levels of productivity. Then worries begin, and management wants to know why workers are not up to par. While this may work for industry, it does not provide a good analogy to classrooms.

First, industrial goals are usually very precise. Costs are recorded, materials measured, workers paid, and profits generated from the product. Furthermore, there is a product that can be judged in value, a number placed upon it. Education is more like a service industry in that performance is the product, one not always easily measured in numbers. Services—and teaching is, after all, a service industry—may have more varied goals than customer satisfaction. The service itself can be reduced to a valuation, but the performance may be open to interpretation. Different services may have evolved out of antithetical goals and objectives.

For example, a physical therapist seeking to alleviate a sports injury is both a teacher and a diagnostician. Ultimately, customer satisfaction is important, but it will take a long time before the customer knows if the goal has been achieved. In addition, the customer must cooperate with the therapist for a successful result. Customer and therapist are actor and audience, working together for the result. Poor skills or motivation on either side or both sides will retard progress. Growth will be slow and sporadic. Measurements of flexibility can be very precise, but the reasons for success or failure may not be nearly as clear. Thus, while therapy derives from biological and medical science, the performances of patient and teacher may require a powerful dose of artistry for a cure.

When results are poor, the patient is prone to blame the therapist or doctor. This is very much like the situation in schools, where poorly performing students blame their teachers. Worse yet, if educational leaders imply or promote the notion that poor results stem from subpar input, then the door is open for one-sided criticism of teachers. The audience waits to be treated, and it is up to the teacher/therapist to get a result. Who asks about teacher satisfaction or therapist satisfaction?

Measurement, to be valid, must match goals and treatment, to continue our medical metaphor. Goals must be clear, treatment suited to the audience, and results reasonably interpreted. The more precise the goals and the sharper the measurement, the more likely results will be valid. If the goals for learning number skills are exact, and the teacher's method is effective, a pretest and a posttest of student learning are likely to show growth.

If goals are vague, however, or teaching methods unsuited to subject or audience, results may at best correlate partially with input. Research in education seldom shows a direct line between input and output. There are just too many complex variables interfering, too many intrusions, and too little control. That is why educational research, drawing from scientific method, sets limits, selects samples, and attempts to control each situation. Otherwise, teachers may be drawing erroneous conclusions from results, misunderstanding what these signify. Errors may arise from causes we identify, but may also arise from those we cannot identify. Sometimes, results are confusing, and teachers are not at all sure what were the causes.

For example, a teacher works very hard to get students to understand the relationship between supply and demand in economics. But the formal test of economic understanding yields low scores on supply-and-demand questions. The test questions, it turns out, were mostly of supply-and-demand graphs that frightened students. Upon review, the teacher discovers that the ideas were covered, but she had forgotten to teach how to interpret graphs and charts. Lack of skill trumped knowledge, perhaps.

Thus, a science of measurement supports a science of teaching, but it must be applied and interpreted with care and caution. There are many influences on a lesson, unit, or course, and these can depress or inflate scores. Even when a teacher tries to control all aspects of learning, there may still be outside or internal or personal changes that raise or lower scores. A very well-designed test, appropriately administered under controlled conditions, will yield a good result. Yet teachers and assessors must be cautious in assigning and ranking causes.

An irony of scientific teaching is that outcomes need critical review. Artist teachers interpret results, including measurements, before deciding how much an audience has achieved, much less why. Testing and measurement provide benefits on many levels, guiding teachers in the selection of input and the interpretation of outcomes. But it is very difficult and dangerous to draw direct connections between teacher quality, input, and audience quality, or output. What happens in between must be examined and assessed each step of the way to make a professional judgment. Just as a therapist gets to know her patient, persona and style impact growth and recovery. Confidence in the teacher role contributes as much as exercise in shaping the physical outcome.

Measurement of leg lifts and flexibility demonstrate 50 percent improvement, from 30 percent to 45 percent, but the patient isn't happy. Communication, the basis of teaching, comes to a grinding halt. The patient wants 100 percent results, total flexibility. So the teacher/therapist explains why this isn't possible, and if both work together, a new goal is mutually agreed upon. New instructions to improve are provided, and the patient cooperates. Thus, progress is made. But what if the patients, students, are unwilling or unable to cooperate?

Furthermore, measurement is very much a part of education, and a handmaiden of a science of teaching. Teachers need to read and understand the goals of instruction to interpret outcomes. Control helps identify causes, but these are open to error and to debate. We are not always sure just which factors were key, and which were marginal. Much of the interpretation of research—for example, cooperative learning—depends upon goals that are set. Goals incorporate subject matter and the evolution of audience social skills. Sometimes, as teachers, we under- or overestimate social skills in developing and directing small-group problem solving. Other times, teachers may easily turn problems and content over to a highly skilled group of students who already know each other. This group readily applies principles for carrying out the cooperative venture.

Nevertheless, despite controversy over results, interpretations, and issues, a good deal of work has gone into a scientific basis for instruction. More of this deals with the learning end of the spectrum than with the teaching viewpoint. Much is known about the functioning of memory: the factors that influence long-term and short-term recall of information. A great deal is known about measuring problem solving and assessing the reasoning that enhances higher-order thinking. There is also valuable research on classroom management, social behavior, school atmosphere, administrative practices, and so on. Measurement techniques have been developed for and applied to nearly every aspect of the educational endeavor. Yet when a teacher walks into his or her classroom, choosing a role and interpreting reactions require much more than a set of measures.

DISCOVERY

Teaching as a science can be expressed in many ways. One way is when teachers seek to predict outcomes based on input and audience capabilities. Applying principles from motivation research, teachers design a curriculum that engages the audience, encouraging individual and group inquiry. Students, in essence, reproduce knowledge that is already known. The goal is usually acquisition of content, and that is fine. Then audiences are ready for an examination on the data they have acquired.

Another, quite different, approach is aimed at fostering a sense of discovery and imagination (Egan 1992). This may be defined as audience involvement with the process of a science. Students are learning how to use tools to make discoveries of their own. Usually, this takes the form of working by induction: collecting data and making inferences from raw materials. In effect, audiences participate directly in "hands-on" experimentation. Principles are derived from findings rather than applied to data. Audiences produce their own conclusions.

For example, teachers can present a concept of evolution as a principle to learn. Evolutionary theory is later illuminated by examples and case studies. Predictions are made, and knowledge of both theory and examples from a text is measured on a test and by classroom dialogue. By contrast, students can be asked to infer evolutionary theory or principles by looking at Darwin's drawings of birds or reptiles adapted to different ecologies. Here the data are presented first for audience analysis; this is followed by attempts to generalize from the examples. A process of induction generates analysis and inference.

The point of careful and predictable presentations is mainly to build knowledge. The point of discovery is mainly to enhance insight and promote inventiveness. In a principled approach the outcome sought is growth in terms of measurable content. A discovery approach sets up an atmosphere for invention, inviting insight into the unknown. The two approaches can be integrated to promote a much deeper appreciation of a subject (e.g., evolution, adaptation, and natural selection).

There are two aspects, then, to a science of teaching, induction and deduction—reasoning from data to a generalization, or applying a generalization to data. Neither is right or wrong, but both merge to form a basis for different teaching processes (Chazan and Ball 1995). Inductive reasoning is usually more interactive for an audience, particularly if they have cases to work with in an experimental setting. Deduction is a more orderly and contextual fit of theory to data.

Induction probably lends itself more easily to active hands-on learning, leading to insights—the "aha!" phenomenon. Deduction may be a better fit with lecture and investigative methods, carefully planning and testing a theory. Teachers choose their methods based on the content they want to get across and audience potential. Reproduction of knowledge is a good base for inference, but it tends to reinforce memorization and terminology, not analysis and synthesis. A discovery approach appeals to a novice as an exciting journey into the unknown. The learner gets to make the discovery, with guidance, but without answers supplied by the teacher/actor. A rich learning environment with lots of data, equipment, and hands-on experiences promotes tinkering and insights that lead to discoveries. Students begin to extend insights into new areas, and perhaps concoct new ideas and make inventions.

A science of teaching by discovery dovetails well with artistic approaches. The intersection of artistry and science in teaching leads to personal experiences that build interest in a subject. These interests, once formed, may grow into a real passion for learning a particular field or topic, a level of seriousness that most teachers respect and treasure. Society is conflicted about what it really wants from education: lots of knowledge or lots of creativity. Leaders demand that teachers bring students up to adequate content levels but also demand that students know how to reason and think critically. This quandary extends to every subject and every grade, kindergarten to college.

For example, citizens must know their historical roots and be familiar with political systems. Young citizens are socialized to be active and responsible, to uphold the system yet be able to protest its injustices. Art students should know the history of art and also be able to produce (not just reproduce) art of their own. Science students should memorize the periodic table of the elements but also be able to conduct their own research study on heavy metals. In short, different strains of artistic and scientific teaching are expressed as competing rather than complementary goals. Dichotomies divide teachers and audiences into antagonistic camps with different learning processes.

But a science and an art of teaching overlap in supporting richer and more insightful learning. This learning fuses lower- and higher-level thinking with rich knowledge bases to foster imagination and discovery as well as good test results on content.

AUDIENCE PARTICIPATION

1. How would you define science in teaching?
2. Does educational psychology help in managing students?
3. Are students predictable?
4. Do test scores really matter? Do test scores count as science in guiding your judgments about success or failure?
5. How might you use the science of teaching to change, guide, or shape your daily lessons, units, and courses?

CONCLUSION AND CODA

There is a great deal of evidence to show that students tend to master subjects with far more depth when they feel motivated and interested than when they are bored or angry (Sternberg 1988). This entirely reasonable finding is supported by quite a large number of studies, but must still be translated to individual classrooms. Motivation is a "hot" topic in educational research, with many variations in experimentation to discover how teachers promote or inhibit student motivation.

We would also like to know how the art and science of teaching can combine to improve attention, bolster energy, and sustain interest. Usually the artistic role produces more ideas on how to engage and stimulate audiences than the scientific. Stage and team metaphors open up new ways to arouse individuals and groups from slumber. Meanwhile, educational research helps teachers think about case studies that provide guidance on how to motivate students to learn, and how to overcome "blockages" and disinterest.

Drawing upon both the flamboyant and dramatic, as well as detailed observation and assessment, provides a sharing of roles, each of which provides different kinds of feedback to teachers. An industrial model provides for overall organization and measurement techniques to assess student productivity.

Scientific research also reveals that cooperative learning or group work, primarily student-to-student communication, can be very effective in some settings. Group action can perhaps be more powerful than direct instruction (Slavin 1990). However, studies also show that in some teachers' hands, cooperative learning becomes a catchall for students to work together ad hoc. The teacher can have some time off to grade papers, and that the outcomes lack focus and specificity. In some situations students avidly pursue the assigned or initiated goals that have been set. In others, they waste time on personal conversation and petty gossip.[8]

In deciding what works, whether science or art or a combination, much depends on the goals set and the expectation of a cooperative learning strategy (Slavin 2008). Materials properly presented for problem solving can enhance group achievement. A lack of resources or a misapplied theory can turn into a big waste of time. Groups need real material to work with and motivating questions to struggle over.

An intersection of roles enriches the teacher. This persona is using artistic means to dramatize content, and scientific means to choose effective techniques, as well as diagnose reactions. Great artists can work alone, but rarely achieve an effect through ego alone: They also have studied the subject intensively and must understand human psychology to achieve their objectives.

Finally, as always in education, a great deal of power rests with the interaction between teacher roles and audience roles. Artistry informs and projects, while science measures and predicts. The richest forms of teaching grow out of achieving a balance between every aspect of the artistic and scientific, fusing the "art" of social skills with a grasp of human psychology to foster growth and imagination.

AN INTERVIEW ABOUT YOUR THINKING SO FAR: ART AND SCIENCE

1. Is an artistic role valuable for classroom teaching? Why?
2. Is a scientific role valuable for classroom teaching?
3. Are both art and science equally valuable?
4. Are both drama and psychological research equally valuable?
5. What qualities do you think make "great" teachers? Are these more related to their personae, or their grasp of scientific principles?
6. What kinds of teachers have you enjoyed more: those who are dramatic and energetic, or those who are clear, logical, and diagnostic?
7. Do you agree or disagree that a balance, a fusing, of roles is better than emphasizing one over the other? Why?

NOTES

1. Josephine Miles, "Center," in *Collected Poems, 1930–83* (Champaign: University of Illinois Press, 1983).

2. Zevin, recording from Bayside High School, twelfth-grade classroom, June 4, 2009. Used with the permission of the school, teacher, and students.

3. Eisner (1993). A major proponent of teaching as an art provides insights for achieving this ideal.

4. Grasha (1996). A book for those who hope to be stylish teachers and remain memorable in students' minds.

5. Stigler and Hiebert (1999). In this book, two researchers offer ideas and more about what all teachers can do in their classrooms to achieve a fusion of the art and science of teaching.

6. Perkins (1981). The book presents an interesting discussion of how people are stimulated to undertake serious and creative thinking.

7. May 8, 2009. Used with the permission of the school, faculty, and students.

8. U.S. Department of Education (1987). This is a compilation of research findings applied to teaching and learning, but who has read it?

4

Content and Process

"Now, what I want is, Facts. Teach these boys and girls nothing but Facts. Facts alone are wanted in life. Plant nothing else, and root out everything else. You can only form minds of reasoning animals upon Facts: nothing else will ever be able to be of any service to them . . . This is the principle on which I bring up these children. Stick to the Facts, sir!"

The scene was a plain, bare, monotonous vault of a schoolroom, and the speaker's square forefinger emphasized his observations by underscoring every sentence with a line on the schoolmaster's sleeve. The emphasis was helped by the speaker's square wall of a forehead, which had eyebrows for its base, while his eyes found commodious cellarage in two dark caves, overshadowed by the wall . . .

The speaker, and the schoolmaster, and the third grown person present, all backed away a little, and swept with their eyes the inclined plane of little vessels then and there arranged in order, ready to have imperial gallons of facts poured into them until they were full up to the brim.

—Charles Dickens, *Hard Times*[1]

A pedagogy of mutuality presumes that all human minds are capable of holding beliefs and ideas which, through discussion and interaction, can be moved toward some shared frame of reference. Both child and adult have points of view, and each is encouraged to recognize the other's though they may not agree. They must come to recognize that differing views are based on recognizable reasons and that these reasons provide the basis for adjudicating rival beliefs.

Sometimes you are "wrong," sometimes others are—
that depends on how well reasoned the views are. Sometimes
opposing views are both right—or both wrong. The child is
not merely ignorant nor an empty vessel, but somebody able
to reason, to make sense, both on her own and through discourse with others.

—Jerome Bruner, *The Culture of Education*[2]

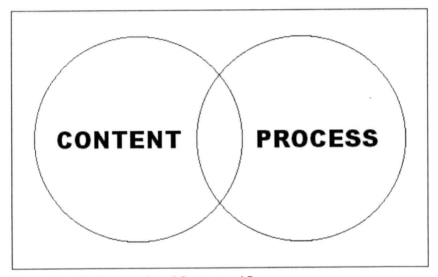

Figure 4.1.   The Intersection of Content and Process

Every teacher plays the role of knowledge giver. Teachers offer students knowledge in many forms and quantities.[3] This knowledge,
content, or subject matter is a communication that includes words,
images, sounds, and artifacts. Content is the stuff of teaching. It can
be perceived as inherently interesting, confusing, or dull, or perhaps a
mixture of all three reactions. How content is presented can make a
huge difference in how it is received.

Process is the method of delivery, how the content is presented.
Teachers may present content using different media, through varying
styles, and by drawing from many philosophies of teaching and learning (Fenstermacher 1990). Student understanding and perception of
both content and process are deeply and often unconsciously shaped
by the teacher's approach.

Content is usually viewed as mainly cognitive and informational,
the stuff of your basic lesson. However, content may inadvertently or
purposely send emotional messages along with data. The facts may

communicate a good deal of values and feelings in a combination that may be obscured by the delivery of data. In effect, process, the manner of presenting data, may directly or indirectly also send out reasons, feelings, and interpretations rather than bare facts.

Every teacher supplies knowledge of a subject through a medium of expression, a process, a way of instructing, or, if you will, a method. A teacher cannot really supply content without a process, nor perform a process based on no data at all. Where the two join, at a "pivot point" balancing presentation and content, students gain a sense of learning knowledge and a sense of sources.

The merging of content and process is vitally important for teaching and learning. This is the point at which students connect with both the information presented and the form of communication. For example, a group process in which teams invent and tell stories using a list of metaphors teaches very different skills than individual storytelling. Neither lesson is necessarily "better" than the other; it depends on what teachers want to communicate about metaphors.

A group assignment often encourages cross-checking of usage and syntax, while an individual assignment allows for more individual creativity. Much depends on how familiar students are with social interaction. If students have a good grasp of social relations, then the group process will certainly help them gain a better understanding. However, if students are quiet researchers and observers, then they may benefit more from self-directed inventiveness.

Every lesson, unit, or course combines content and process, presentation and data, and sources and methods—all affecting student learning outcomes.

THE CHARACTERISTICS OF CONTENT

Knowledge, content, and subject matter can range from low-level facts or opinions all the way up to sophisticated ideologies and evaluations. Content can range across statistics, concepts, attitudes, disciplines, topics, information, material objects, and so on. All constitute some form of evidence: the basis for lower- and higher-level thinking.

Content is often viewed as totally factual in nature, requiring basically memorization. Many teachers present information and information-collection systems for storage in our minds. For example, how many of us were asked to memorize the table of the elements, Lincoln's Gettysburg Address, the formula for quadratic equations, the definition of a verb, or the features of Doric, Ionic, and Corinthian art styles?

Content can, however, vary enormously in presentation, depth, quality, and quantity. Data can be presented as the lowest-level laundry list of statistics, addresses, names, or dictionary definitions. But information may also rise to middle levels of application and reasoning, then to the highest levels of synthesis or theory on any given subject.

Learners and teachers do not always recognize where they are in the hierarchy of content. They often disregard or misperceive the difficulty inherent in a presentation of content. For example, many charts, graphs, or maps contain vast amounts of information, often presented as abstract numbers or diagrams. Skills need to be formed to "read" or view this content; otherwise students will lack comprehension and teachers will be frustrated.

Sometimes, the nature of the communication may appear quite factual, but its underpinnings and deeper meaning may affect and shade how students react to the material as a whole (Jones and Vesilind 1994). For example, difficult historical and social issues like the Holocaust, genocide, and slavery may be delivered in quite a matter-of-fact style that students seem to absorb, yet they are disturbed and upset in ways that are not immediately visible.

Many weeks, months, or even years later, the students remember not so much the data of the subject but the emotional charge that was attached to it. The simple facts may induce a deeply held antipathy or sympathy to the topic as a whole, though not necessarily in the direction the teacher intended. Perhaps the way the content was presented needed redesign?

Content, whether factual, analytical, theoretical, or ethical, is usually viewed on much the same level by an audience. Memorization training is a key to acquiring and holding onto content. Facts are facts unless the teacher/actress/actor invigorates reception by a process that engages and enlivens. This is where process enters into its role as a complement and partner to content. Clearly, a teacher must select a process of delivery for the material in the curriculum. That process should support and enhance the material for the audience rather than seem at odds with the instructional goals.

THE CHARACTERISTICS OF PROCESS

Process has two important components: its methodological and social elements. A teacher must choose a form for dealing with the material.

This can be auditory, visual, or written, or a combination of all three—word, image, and sound. Next, teachers must choose from a range of presentation styles: straightforward simple lecture, discussion and/or debate, and role-play, including drama, simulation, or improvisation. Lastly, teachers must decide on an overall method that sets the goals for a lesson, unit, or course.

Many roles are available, from teacher-centered to student-centered, from playing the authority to structured and shared inquiry. Audiences can be organized to receive content by arranging them in smaller or larger units; by treating them as individuals or as groups, large, medium, or small, or as players in a game, role-play, or experiment.

The quantity and quality of content and the process of delivery shape a teacher's decision about how to approach an audience to maximize their receptivity and comprehension. For example, some topics, such as wars or evolution, are complex and need definition. St. Augustine's concept of a "just war," for instance, can be studied purely on a cognitive basis—why wars have happened and what the rules were. But the idea of rules of war also suggests a deep ethical and moral dimension, encouraging a process of debate and argument. Perhaps this lesson is best done in a formal debate-society arrangement?

The concept of evolution can be discussed in purely theoretical terms. Or it can be presented as a record of change using fossils and living fauna, drawing from Darwin's work. Evolution can be turned into a mystery to solve, or simply explained in a straightforward lecture. How the audience will respond is not always predictable.

For a sharing of emotional content, the actress/actor/teacher may wish to arrange students into panels, or small groups. Each will write out their views, present these to classmates, and then discuss what might or might not be the best response to the key questions. Thus, a complex reading is interpreted, with students benefiting from a social exercise that enhances interpretational skills.

The point is this: Content is the stuff of teaching, but it must be delivered through a medium of exchange to an audience able to receive the goods. The data may vary greatly in terms of quality, quantity, degree of fascination, and emotional charge. Every teacher has to deliver content by a process—a channel, approach, method, technique, medium, or strategy. The process is applied to an audience at widely different stages of development and knowledge levels.

Some may still be at the "concrete" reasoning stage, for instance, while others are well into abstract thinking. Mismatches between content and process, between delivery and audience, represent one of the reasons teaching is so difficult and exhausting. The teacher needs a sound diagnosis of the audience to ensure a modicum of successful communication.

Process, then, is the way in which a teacher decides to deliver content, to give it meaning and organization. A teacher's choice of delivery (e.g., lecture, discussion, simulation, role-play) should match the type, quantity, and quality of the content. If there is a mismatch between content and process, the student audience will find the material confusing, frustrating, or downright mystifying. This will result in feelings of inadequacy and lack of self-confidence about the ability to succeed with work. Participation will decline, and possibly a dislike for the body of knowledge will be imparted.

Here again, a good proportion of negative reactions can probably be avoided if the strategy fits the content, and content and strategy fit the audience. However, this is not always easy to decide for a teacher. Much depends upon an audience's initial and continuing reactions to a body of content. Teachers must maintain a keen watch over student feedback to assess the level of performance. If students seem to "get" the ideas presented, then the teacher can upgrade the questions; if not, then levels need to be lower.

For instance, a group of investors may sit and listen to a series of stock and bond analyses that would bore a group of youngsters to death. Having investments at stake, and understanding the delivery system for information, the investors quickly grasp what is happening and appreciate a shared insight. Students who have never watched a stock ticker go by, don't know the symbols, and have no investments at all may be totally mystified. The arcane language and strange numbers flashing by lead to a lack of appreciation for the excitement of others as the market rises or falls dramatically.

A riveting film such as *Wall Street*, a noir mystery or musical, or direct participation in a stock-market game by computer might grip the attention of those who are unfamiliar with economics. Students may feel for the movie characters and their problems. They will want to watch the film epic to find out how the drama ends.

The more gripping and dramatic the presentation, probably the more attentive will be the audience, but much depends on interest and values. Some audiences may mistrust high drama and prefer a calm, measured approach to the knowledge of economics, one that is devoid of emotion and sales pitches. Audience, subject matter, and process must, therefore, be carefully thought out and matched for optimal effects.

BALANCE BETWEEN CONTENT AND PROCESS

As with audience and actor, and theory and practice, there must be a balance between content and process that is mutually supportive and promotes audience engagement. Students feel better about themselves when they are active participants in class or life (Marshall and Weinstein 1984).

Content can itself grip the audience's attention at different levels without the benefit of a teacher-imposed process of delivery. However, this type of content presumes a "ready" audience, one that is already interested in acquiring information or analysis on a subject. For example, if you ask a question in the process of teaching that you think is "easy" (low level), but the student audience sees it as "difficult" (high level), then responses will fall off or disappear altogether (Butler and Newman 1995). You will have to go over the question again and again, becoming a bit frustrated with your audience.

You might also ask a question too early in the process of comprehending and interpreting data, and find few respondents. Many more would have participated if the same question were posed midway or later in the consideration of content. If teacher and audience can meet at the same level, at the same time, in a suitable arrangement, such problems will probably be avoided. Process and content will be fairly well balanced, and audiences will be able to respond quickly and at the level requested by the teacher.

Participation depends on the way a teacher structures audience roles, organizing by individuals or groups to enhance how content is received. The concept of alliances, for example, in foreign-policy studies, may be very sophisticated for youngsters in middle school. However, a teacher might decide to present the idea of political alliances as an allegory by playing a simulation game, arranging students in "nation-teams" who have to negotiate for war or peace through a process of exchanging ideas with one another.

Classroom action would provide a sense of immediacy and play, raising the number of those who would actively join the game. A geometry lesson could translate abstract ideas into building models out of sticks or paper, a hands-on activity. As excitement built, almost every group member would play or work along, effortlessly learning and having fun to boot.

Content that is inherently interesting to an audience "sells" well, and requires relatively little in the way of process to draw interest. Interest is evident from the start, a wonderfully appealing situation for an actress/actor/teacher to experience. A well-educated, motivated audience with an interest in literature will relish a lecture by someone who is a famous author though a poor speaker. The audience will overcome process issues and communication problems by compensating for the delivery in favor of content.

Just as interesting content may sustain the attention of an audience, so process ensures wide and active participation. A famous expert's lecture can sustain the interest of a knowledgeable group that is hungry for knowledge.

By contrast, an audience out for a good time may value the speaker's style and eloquence more than the content, and settle for a demonstrative talk with a dose of good humor. Audience is critically important to reception of content, and an audience may derail or disappoint a speaker who pays no attention to process. A dramatic delivery or presentation through media or role-play lowers the bar of audience attention and encourages participation by greater numbers. They too, have a part to play, a role in the drama.

Process may rivet attention because of its unusual features, dramatic technique, sense of mystery, or emotional issues. The process itself may sell content; here "the medium becomes the message," to use Marshal McLuhan's (1967) famous dictum.[4] For example, young people, usually male, derive great pleasure from computer games that demand skill in battle, auto racing, mountain climbing, or some other dangerous (virtual) pleasure. Games that express power and control with varying degrees of realism provide for a way to engage students who lack interest. Images of the warrior, usually very muscular and sleek, pull the player/audience into a process that is theater.

These examples make the point that content and process are not the same, and are not always equal in attracting an audience. In the business world, much funding and attention is spent on finding out just what sort of content (or product) will sell best, and through which media. In educational circles, we spend a great deal of out time working out ways of more effectively imposing an inherited body of knowledge and content on unwilling subjects. We do not usually check out what the audience already knows, or what they are interested in knowing.

We assume the job of authorities and deliver what audiences need to know, with sometimes less than satisfying results in terms of participation or test outcomes. Content may be offered in ways the audience finds boring and meaningless. But we are here, as teachers, to decide what is best for the audience, not to listen to their advice or reactions, right? We avoid market research in making a sale. For instance, just try forcing a group of eighth graders to listen to a lecture on the Pierce administration or the rules of grammar!

At peak performance, a teacher joins interesting and meaningful content with an exciting and engaging process. This "win-win" situation takes planning and deep knowledge of an audience and a subject. If it works well, results include knowledge growth and highly motivated student behavior. Students seek out answers on their own, asking their own thoughtful questions. They produce work that is above and beyond their assignment in quantity, or quality, or both. As teachers, we yearn for this situation, but usually don't quite know how to make it happen regularly. We don't always consider the deep connections between content and process roles that promote engaging teaching and quality learning. We don't adapt presentations and content to the audience. Decisions are often based on packaged or canned lessons handed down to us from others, or demanded by the school, city, or state curriculum. Worse yet, we repeat our own "tried-and-true" presentations even though we may be tired of them ourselves.

Choice of content and choice of process should work hand in hand by identifying content that complements instructional processes. Two big questions raised in this chapter are how to choose or shape content to support a process of delivery, and how to choose a process that supports the content. In other words, how can content be chosen to maximize interest? And how can a method or instructional approach be selected to enliven and revitalize the information received by the audience?

What is the best fit between content and process to enhance and sustain learning?

AUDIENCE PARTICIPATION

1. What kind of content arouses interest?
2. Which teaching processes or methods encourage engagement?
3. What combination of content and process builds audience participation most?

THE ROLE OF CONTENT

All information may be viewed as content: subject matter, topics, disciplines, databases, and websites—in other words, input into the students' mental landscapes. Feedback provides input into the teacher's mental landscape. In effect, teachers and students are exchanging content and reactions with each other.

Content comes in many sizes and shapes, ranging across subjects we have divided for formal learning purposes into separate entities: mathematics, science, history, art, music, and literature. Content may also be offered as a set of skills: learning to paint, driving an auto, plumbing, weight training, self-improvement, or vocational development.

Thus, content may also grow out of a historically active discipline that represents an accumulated source of knowledge and theory, built on research and evidence. Some fields (e.g., mathematics and history) may go back a long way in time, to the ancient world, even to the earliest written records. Others, such as quantum mechanics, cognitive psychology, or electronic music, may be recent developments.

Disciplines are formal compilations of definitions, ideas, research tools, methodologies, and discoveries. Subject matter and goals are shared by a set of practitioners who organize what is known into categories and structures. Some of us outside our fields may find this knowledge difficult or nearly incomprehensible, like a foreign language. This is often because of the technicalities or theoretical constructs peculiar to one subject. Thus, content can be viewed as topical or disciplinary, with knowledge and theories divided into specialties.

Scholars in a field who offer their findings and methods to others through books, through media, or on the Net are acting as teachers for a variety of audiences. An audience of experts or novices may be sharing their specialty. The highly educated from different fields may be picking up new ideas. Ordinary citizens or students work to grasp the basics of a subject for some personal goal, or to meet local, state, or national requirements.

Naturally, those who seek enlightenment of their own volition are more likely to be better students, more challenging and questioning, than those upon whom a subject is imposed.

The teacher or teaching medium acts as the interpreter of the field for an audience of learners. But the audience may present problems, lack of knowledge, lack of skill, or lack of interest.[5]

Each discipline or field also has a body of research tools that are used to make sense of the evidence that is discovered, compiled, and collected. Each discipline has a body of collected knowledge, methods, and theories that organize the content. Within a field, there are usually differences of opinion, and differences in interpretations and theories. Scholars may have fierce debates about the goals, meaning, and application of their fields.

These contests and conflicts may, however, be too esoteric for the general-public view. Even classroom teachers of a subject may be unaware of or unclear about internal debates. Some views of content may harden into ideological stands that color much of the data that enters a field, for example, "new" math. Because of disputes over interpretations of content, we may not be entirely sure about how to understand and apply our knowledge to our students. Therefore, teachers may need to leave content open and negotiable rather than completely fixed for the ages.

Content from the disciplines may also be viewed in terms of the quantity of information available and the quality of interpretation and explanation. Information, factual evidence, provides the basic input we need to know: dates, names, places, numbers, statistics, personal identification numbers, and passwords. We place these data in our memories or electronic storage for future reference. Information alone is only a basic platform for performing higher-level functions.

Higher-level thinking is what helps us solve complex problems, ranging from understanding and interpretation to synthesis and evaluation. These higher-level thinking skills are shared by all human beings to some degree, and can be honed and developed.

Content can be classified or categorized in a variety of ways—for example, on a scale using a schema like Bloom's (1956) cognitive domain (i.e., recall, comprehension, application, analysis, synthesis, and evaluation). Or it can be viewed in terms of disciplines (e.g., science, mathematics, social studies, art, music, literature, and language). Both the categories and the subjects can be further broken down into smaller and smaller categories or fields for students to study (e.g., algebra, ecological history). Categories and subjects are open to permutation and adaptation.

However, categories may not always produce clear distinctions about which content is appropriate or needed. If you ask for a definition of *poverty*, just what level of answer will you encounter? From a taxonomic point of view, this is a comprehension question. However, if students have recently memorized a definition of poverty and repeat that, then isn't that simply recall? If you thoughtfully think over several definitions and provide a new one, is that application a higher-level answer? If you come up with a completely new definition based on critical review of five books in the field on poverty, you are operating at a very high level and have invented a synthesis of your own.

Despite these difficulties, the point is to develop a system for thinking about content along a scale from the easier to the moderate to the more difficult to teach and to learn. If you apply a category system (consisting of levels) to content, you will get some idea of measuring quality. Classifying content into a lower-, middle-, and higher-level problem can be further defined in terms of Bloom's Cognitive Taxonomy (1956) or some other system.

The point is that content can be viewed, from an analytical perspective, as requiring greater or lesser problem-solving capability. Content may also be viewed from a subject-matter perspective as a body of evidence—a set of data, investigative methods, and conclusions. There are many ways of presenting content through process: lecture, debate, role-play, conversation, and gaming. Whatever body of knowledge is serving as the main course for learning and teaching, some strategy or method of presentation is employed in delivering the data to the audience. A central pivot point revolves around the teacher's philosophy of knowledge: Is treatment of the subject matter "fixed," to be absorbed, or is it "open," to be questioned and discussed?

AUDIENCE PARTICIPATION

1. Can content, subject matter, facts, and so on provide inherent interest?
2. What sort of content, in your view, generates interest? What sort does not?
3. Do lists provide interest? Do theories? Do stories? Do formulas?
4. What sort of content and subject matter does everyone need to know to survive?
5. What sort of content would you like to teach most? Least? Why?

THE ROLE OF PROCESS

Process encompasses the behaviors, strategies, techniques, and methods a teacher uses to communicate knowledge, ideas, and values to an audience. These ways of communicating grow out of a theory of instruction and a philosophy. Teachers consciously or subconsciously adopt a theory and philosophy when they make a choice in planning any lesson, what is taught and how it is taught.[6] In other words, teachers decide to present content in a particular way, choosing a format that makes sense of their subject and meets the needs and interests of their audience.

Teachers also make choices about the curriculum based on the process they intend to use to get information and ideas across. Sometimes the content will, in their minds, generate the method of delivery. On other occasions, the process will shape the content selection. Either way, it is impossible to deliver process without content, or content without process, although in many areas of education, people try to get away with this by dominating communication with emotion.

A STORY ABOUT PROCESS AND SCIENCE

A noted physicist was asked to teach atomic theory to a group of middle-school students, and he was told to help them understand how particles interacted, but *not* to "dumb down" the lesson. Maybe he could throw in the ideas of fusion and fission, too? He was a bit taken aback since he usually worked with a college audience that presumably had several years of science and mathematics under their belts, as well as being able to understand science lingo.

Well, being a bright guy, and someone highly conscious of process as well as content in his own courses, he devised a dramatic delivery for the young people.

He herded the student audience into a large room filled with piles of Ping-Pong balls, placed them in different positions, and gave them popguns that shot more Ping-Pong balls. He asked them to predict what would happen if they fired into the stacked piles, even to the extent of where the balls would move.

Each student studied the room and wrote a prediction, with a chart included.

Then he told the students to start firing Ping-Pong balls, all of which shot into the neat piles, driving balls madly across and around the room and past students' heads and feet. As they laughed and fired away, many later reported that they got the idea of particles knocking into each other, blasting each other away, and that when all were firing at the same time, it was a kind of chaos, and fun, and funny. "And so, professor, was that fusion or fission?" they asked. And he said, "If you got the idea of particles, you get the idea of fusion and fission—so why not look it up?"

A process approach to teaching may privilege method over content, but does not *ideally* either degrade or devaluate the information. Each and every player in the teaching role must communicate through some method, even if the teacher is a machine. Some audiences enjoy talking to a machine (computer), and the machine can act authoritatively or democratically, much as a live model, by working with or providing for students. Even proverbial "couch potatoes," sitting watching rather mindless, "touchy-feely" TV commercials, take in information and make (perhaps) subliminal decisions about shopping.

Of course, process-content matches sometimes fail even the advertisers, and many audiences are unsure what the message is about. They are entangled in emotions, or unclear about the goal because they are absorbed in the tone or action of the message rather than its selling point. A more allegorical message with heavy emotion will more likely be misinterpreted in terms of its intent than a simple, straightforward sales pitch. If miscommunication occurs, the advertiser/teacher will have wasted a good deal of money and effort in arranging the communication.

In much the same way as advertisers, teachers make strategic errors in the way they present data. Often there is simply far too much content to absorb at one time. Sometimes teachers generalize so abstractly that the content soars over the audience's heads. They may offer so much detail that the audience loses track of the sum of the parts. Now and then, content gets lost in an open-ended discussion or game. Controversial issues may be swept away by emotions. Here, too, a teacher may waste a great deal of time and effort on communication, but get little in the way of learning results.

Who said teaching was easy, and who said balance was simple? Basically, whether it's live, recorded, or electronic, there are two major choices in the delivery of content, depending upon which goal has priority:

1. a philosophical commitment to mastery of a defined subject or topic, its absorption and comprehension
2. a philosophical commitment to mastery of the tools of inquiry for a subject or topic, its application and analysis

Focusing on matter or inquiry is a pivotal choice for a teacher. A great deal of the process or methods selected for communication will be determined by short- or long-term goals that emphasize an "asking" or a "telling" mode. Teachers who see themselves as communicators whose end product is primarily knowledge will tend to be didactic.

They will stress processes like lecture, recitation, and research. Teachers who see their end product as primarily conceptual will tend to stress processes that are analytical. Typically, these teachers will employ discussion, discovery, and debate.

Knowledge transmitters will also often prefer to work with students as individuals and to encourage self-study, while inquirers may give much more play to groups and cooperative-learning techniques. By the way, a teacher's choice is often based on deeply held, historically supported, culturally rooted traditions. Depending on their experiences and practice, and their sense of authority or democracy, teachers opt for processes that fit the role they see for themselves.

In terms of process, many teachers see a match, a mutually supportive fit, of techniques and topics to school mores. For example, cooperative learning tends to be popular among alternative-school teachers and those in charge of younger children, and less frequently used in comprehensive high schools. However, it seems to me that delivery by means of cooperative learning can suit almost any age or venue. Its value depends upon the goals, subject, and audience you are working with at the time.

Key to the whole decision about which process or delivery system to use in presenting a topic are the goal and subject. A cooperative-learning group effort, for example, might be more effective for researching a science experiment than a lengthy instructor lecture. If, however, a teacher had "set up" the experiment for student investigation to reach a precise set of right answers, then a lecture would probably have been more efficient in reaching that goal.

A cooperative-learning format stressing an inquiry, discovery, problem-solving approach could be designed for the very same science topic, but with a more open-ended and experimental conclusion. Process depends upon the goal and whether it is open or closed ended. Once a content goal is set (i.e., memorization or investigation), the means of getting there will become apparent, by lecture, cooperative learning, self-study, or simulation.

Cooperative learning can also, if handled in a rigid, prescriptive manner, divide students into far too many groups for a teacher to monitor. This results in a great deal of wasted time and effort as students gossip and wander, rather than sticking to the task at hand. A great deal depends upon the way audiences view the process, as valuable or as trivial, as work or as play, as socializing or as sharing ideas.

Thus, there is a basic issue of authority versus democracy on the part of all players in a teaching process. The parenting, coaching, or guiding process can also be shaped by how heavy-handedly or freely the leader acts. Leaders, teachers, parents, administrators—all those who play the guiding role—have a tendency, particularly in difficult situations or with problematic audiences, to revert to a stance of authority. Authority can undercut and even destroy a message of "distributed" decision making and sharing of ideas.

A beautiful process can become repressive in the hands of a driving, demanding, and controlling leader. In sum, a balanced approach in which content and process marry nicely is the goal. We seek quality and quantity that are matched to audience attention and ability. The overall goal of balance is one that is much advised but not easily attained without a good deal of trial-and-error experimentation, field testing, and analysis of results.

AUDIENCE PARTICIPATION

1. How important do you think process is in presentations?
2. Do color, mood, style, meaning, staging, and delivery count, really count?
3. And which factors count for most in getting your message across?
4. If teaching is a process, would it be better if it were more like a performance, or less like a performance? Why?
5. Does process also contribute content?
6. For instance, is a skill a process if taught as a list of directions?
7. Is a skill a process if taught as a hands-on approach, as an experiment?
8. Can process be imposed by the teacher/leader/guide? Why or why not?

Process, the means for delivering material in a given subject, can be thought of as aiming for either definite conclusions to be memorized, or as tentative conclusions that stimulate inquiry and argument. Your choice of process as a teacher, and the way it is carried out, should fit your goals for presenting a subject. The actual functioning procedure is what counts, rather than the label applied, such as discussion, debate, cooperative learning, role-play, or lecture.

Building a process, however creative, that continually is measured by achievement in content misses the point. If testing seeks improvements in amounts, sizes, lists, scores, recollections, and encyclopedic knowledge, the teaching needs to match the goals. Where the overall philosophy demands mainly right answers and wrong answers, this invariably creates a quest for knowledge, leaving little or no margin for error or doubt, interpretation or controversy. Such a view of content as accurate or inaccurate promotes didactic instruction. Methods of delivery can consist of simple lectures, recitations, and memorization.

In terms of educational psychology, answers are set and the audience is responsible for learning what has already been handed down as accurate and truthful. Truth is a given, and discussion focuses on understanding rather than insight or interpretation. By contrast, building a process measured by questioning of content, seeking evidence, and checking conclusions yields more provocative instructional methods. Reviewing arguments and debating issues sets a tone and mood of probability and discussion.

There are more probable and less probable answers, not precisely right and wrong answers. This invariably creates a quest for meaningfulness in terms of reasoning, leaving room for doubt and error. In fact, error and doubt add to process by creating openings for inquiry. Learners, the audience, are invited to contribute conclusions. In this process, answers are open to checking and are not wholly settled, but open to revision.

Therefore, process can be thought of less in terms of the overt method of delivery (e.g., lecture, discussion, cooperative learning, debate) and more in terms of performance.

The overall experience of teaching may encourage critical thinking and the consideration of alternatives, or build to a settled conclusion. Always, the ultimate outcome for the audience should be kept firmly in the forefront of process. In a good marriage content and process are neatly balanced, neither dominating the other. Is the outcome determined, known, and certain, or is the outcome indeterminate and uncertain?

STYLES OF TEACHING: DIRECT, INDIRECT, AND NONDIRECT

In conclusion, our teaching style, the way we treat content and process, is deeply influenced by our philosophy and psychology of instruction. Much depends on whether we see content as proved, factual, and complete or as open to challenge and revision. Questioning facts, analyzing theories, and debating issues demand openness. Thus, we would logically expect a "Socratic" or inquiry teacher to encourage discussion and debate in many forms.

For those seeking a goal of disseminating factual knowledge, we might expect a more direct style of lecture. However, life being what it is, in the complex world of teaching, audience, and curriculum, teachers invariably mix goals and styles. It is from content, and standards, that different performance styles develop to suit the goals.

For example, the more known and certain the goals, the more direct the style of instruction. The more mysterious and critical the goals, the more the style of teaching will be open and indirect. The locus of teacher control tends to sacrifice content for process in a directive mode, and process for content in a nondirective mode.

Performance can be characterized on a sliding scale, from directive, to direct, through indirect, to nondirect. At each point on the continuum, the teaching process shifts.

Behaviors change to suit the goals: more or fewer activities, more or less lecture, more or less group discussion. In effect, teachers alter their methods to suit what they see as a more effective and efficient delivery of content.

Direct Instruction

Direct instruction immediately brings to mind the all-too-typical teaching pattern that is composed of lecturing and asking specific questions with detailed answers from an audience. The teacher is in nearly total control of the process, which is basically unequal communication from an expert to novices. Communication is on a subject that the individual or group is supposed to absorb up to a specific standard for successful achievement.

Feedback from the audience tends to be limited and brief, although there may be a few annoying queries now and then. The learning community is engaged in concurrent deliberations with their leader, sharing ideas and views as individuals in a group. Direct-teaching processes tend to promote the teacher as the arbiter of conclusions. Student summaries usually memorize the content to reach a conclusion that has already been planned. Audiences tend to have very little control over either the story or its direction.

Members may often comment upon, add interpretations to, or subtract interpretations from the overall narrative. However, despite these potential drawbacks, direct instruction can be both effective and enjoyable. For instance, listening to an entertaining expert lecture on a particular topic can be a rewarding experience. A knowledge base is built or reinforced, and understanding a topic is enhanced. However, there is not much opportunity for interaction, clarification, or elaboration.

Politically, direct instruction is a model based on a strong leader. In some instances, the leader can be self-appointed, in the sense of a teacher who takes control by dint of personality, expertise, or drama. A group of followers emerges, and they energize and support the leader by working toward the goals set out for them. They can work alone or together.

In a direct teaching process, individuals have limited autonomy to make decisions. They do have some input on issues of agenda, curriculum, pacing, or direction. But they have relatively little to say about overall program or purpose. As you can see, a political metaphor works fairly well for classroom/teaching operations, in terms of "direct" democracy.

Perhaps classrooms in the direct mode might best be likened to a situation involving a strong mayor or a Supreme Court justice, while what we will call an indirect mode might be termed distributed, or limited, democracy. At a more extreme end of the range, direct instruction might be more like a dictatorship or tyranny than a situation involving a reasonable, rule-oriented leader.

Indirect Instruction

Indirect instruction brings to mind a less typical, though common, teaching pattern of asking questions and fostering the expression of students' ideas. Moving a discussion forward to a goal of shared understanding is a basic goal of indirect process. The teacher, as actress/actor, is still much in control of this process, but not totally. Although it may not look that way to many in the student audience, indirect teachers' questioning is subtle and skillful, and conversation occurs almost as a casual give-and-take of ideas.

Feedback tends to be much greater for indirect than for direct teaching because extended interaction is more valued. Students communicating to the instructor, and to each other, form a community. One might say that indirect teaching encourages audiences to collaborate on the formation, and justification, of responses. Students and teacher work together to reach a partial or full consensus—a majority or minority agreement on views.

There may be a good deal of student-to-student conversation as well as teacher-to-student, student-to-teacher discussion. The teacher respectfully remains on the sidelines when a good argument erupts, nodding approvingly for interesting remarks and good reasons. However, the indirect instructor does not approve any ideas as better than others, or as correct. In addition, students might have considerable influence, formal and informal, in making policy, choosing homework assignments, and contributing to group activities.

Audiences working through indirect modes share control of the story and its direction with the teacher. The two key role-players work to influence the plot, and to create or alter characters and add or subtract details to suit their own shifting interpretations. Players must take into account the viewpoints of all active community members.

To use a political simile, indirect instruction takes on the qualities of a town assembly in a polis, or ancient Greek city-state, with conversations and sometimes conflict between leaders and representatives. However, most teachers, unlike Athenian legislators, are not elected to office. Perhaps we might liken indirect teaching to a U.S. town-hall hearing, or perhaps an enlightened governor working with a legislature, or maybe a courtroom setting with judge, jury, and attorneys. As you can see, there is a sliding scale of metaphors for the many variations of indirect teaching within the overall spectrum of process.

Nondirect Instruction

"Nondirect" instruction may be viewed as the other end of the continuum from the most direct instruction, with indirect in between. Conceptually, nondirect instruction brings to mind situations in which all or almost all of the control and direction over process is handed over to the audience. Participants act either individually or as a group, depending on the educational goals that have been given priority. Priorities are set by negotiation and agreement, not imposition from outside or above. In some cases, there is no leader at all, and none wanted.

Nondirect instruction is not as unusual as you might think, although it is rarer than direct or indirect. In some cases, the teachers are also students; all are one and the same. For example, an election is being conducted and everyone (ideally) has a voice and a vote. In a New England town meeting or an old-fashioned Quaker religious service, all are equal and may speak freely. For a classroom to approach this ideal takes a great deal of development and cooperation, and it is quite possible.

Groups acting together, sharing and exchanging views, and coming to a consensus may be examples of nondirective instruction. This is a situation in which everyone present has input into the final outcome. The exact nature and content is uncertain rather than predetermined. Audiences in effect teach each other and share the evolution of the story based on suggestions from members. Each participant can act as a student or a teacher to develop a coherent plot and finale that will satisfy all or most of the citizen learners.

To use a political simile of legislation, nondirect teaching is democratic or perhaps anarchic on occasion. Nevertheless, a nondirect process is a model of problem solving and negotiation. Discussion could include lectures and debates, role-play and argument, but all in the service of the group's goals, not a director's or individual's goal. An example would be classes or schools where students take real charge of their student governments, conducting elections with only a minimum of teacher supervision.

Thus, process, delivery, and communication, direct, indirect, and nondirect, fall along a continuum of instruction based on different purposes and goals. Among the most important of these are the acquisition of knowledge, and the know-how of problem solving.

Within this context of "certainty" and "uncertainty," of a range of control, from direct to indirect to nondirect, those playing the role of teacher choose one or more balancing rods for their tightrope act, from a repertory of strategies that treat audiences as more or less independent and participatory learners. Clearly, information giving, including dramatics, and reasoning, if presented as correct and accurate, tends to foster the absorption of "given wisdom" and "transmitted ethics."

On the other side, those who choose to emphasize participation and inquiry build in an atmosphere of distributed democracy with mutually supportive cooperative-learning investigations and other forms of cooperative learning that draw people into a process of research and discovery. Such acts will foster skill development as much as, or more than, transmitted information, wisdom, or ethics.

In effect, an indirect or nondirect delivery system creates a more open framework, in which content becomes a vehicle for conversation—not an end in itself, as it is with a direct delivery—

AUDIENCE PARTICIPATION

1. Which delivery system, direct, indirect, or nondirect, would you favor for a bedtime story? Which for a public address to get elected? Which for teaching how to ride a bicycle, make a fire, or paint a kitchen?
2. Which delivery system would you favor in a war?
3. Which delivery system would you favor for driver training?
4. Which delivery system would you favor for geometry, culinary arts, or fencing?

and the teacher is more of a manager and guide for the process than the one drawing the conclusions for the audience.

INTERSECTIONS BETWEEN PROCESS AND CONTENT

Thus, content and process are often viewed separately, as distinct decision-making spheres. But they are actually closely related: a combination of two teacher roles, two decision-making spheres. You might think of content and process as a kind of yin and yang, working in harmony to achieve instructional objectives.

Ideally speaking, there should be a balance between the two forces. Process selection should match content presentation for a maximum effect on audiences. An integrative, relational view ought to produce the greatest increases in learning because of mutual support between the data and the method of delivery.

Theoretically at least, there is a mix of content and process, strategies and data, that has the most powerful impact on the right kind of audience. Maximizing motivation and learning, in both qualitative and quantitative terms, is the highest goal in teaching, but rather difficult to achieve. Teachers need to experiment with "matches" and observe the effects. Higher participation, extended answers, and an atmosphere of excitement are positive signs of active learning.

Content provides information: the database for growth. As the old bromide goes, "Knowledge is power." However, this is potentially true only if an audience is capable of appreciating what it is receiving. Do the new data move them forward or frustrate them? Some of us can appreciate a grand theory of the universe taught by Sir Stephen Hawking, listening for a couple of hours to his lecture. Others might find him difficult to understand and didactic, even if dramatic, because of a lack of ideas and interest in the subject. A hands-on demonstration of physics and astronomy might be just what those people need to spark their interest and attention. A dynamic visual image of the planets spinning around the sun in a sparkling intergalactic setting makes use of media presentation in a way that attracts attention. Even better would be an activity in which students helped to shape the heavens by pushing buttons and maneuvering a spaceship through a representative universe.

The process of delivery, of performance, of instruction, can impact an audience in positive, neutral, or negative ways. As much as a teacher plans, reactions grow out of how that audience feels about a subject and about themselves. Rarely, if ever, are audiences completely neutral to any form of learning and teaching. Even the driest talk has a style, a delivery system, and a goal that is sensed by an audience. The more the participants are attuned to the content, and vice versa, the more they will achieve.

Even the most innovative cooperative-learning technique must incorporate some sort of knowledge base and skills if it is to succeed. Here, too, process is rarely neutral, but shapes content through a delivery system that works in subtle and public ways to either enhance or inhibit learning.

Process and content can take many forms: live, dramatized, textbook, electronic, "hard-copy" paper, speech, or film. Each may have certain advantages for a particular audience, as well as certain drawbacks. No one method/process is likely to provide for all audiences. They, too, must supply a degree of motivation and learning for a combination of processes and content packages to be effective.

Audience and actress/actor must work with content and process to connect. The recent dissemination of electronic teaching and learning does not change overall philosophic or process issues. Rather, electronics give the problems of teaching a new format, one that can be very creative or dull. A vast database that a student must search can be just as boring on a computer as on a blackboard, a SMART Board, or a monitor. Many would rather play a game on their computers because those are interactive, challenging, and engaging, even if trivial.

The point is that content must offer material of interest and some depth combined with a presentation that draws the customers into the lesson. To sustain lessons, there must be something to work on, discuss, and interpret, over and above what an audience already knows. For example, a page out of the telephone book can be quite a boring list to memorize, but it can also be used for a sociological study of names, ethnic distribution, and neighborhood development.

Clear goals and good intentions do not necessarily unite process and content in productive ways. The marriage of content and process, like a successful wedding, must be planned to suit an audience. A teacher must design a lesson to unite skills with examples that are carefully scaffolded to raise the learning bar in small increments. This means that teachers need to diagnose student answers as they go along, strategically raising or lowering the level of questions to match responses. Not an easy skill to acquire, but well worth it!

Methods of delivery can be grouped into direct, indirect, and nondirect styles. Participation is a key: The more students who get involved in thinking aloud, and the deeper their responses, the more likely learning will be greatly enhanced. Most processes, like group work, lecture, drama, debate, discovery, discussion, and so on, are quite familiar to us, although the bottom line seems still to be lecture. Processes can be used in many settings—family, business, sports, TV news, directions—and not just the classroom.

While there are relatively few delivery styles, ranging from very directive to nondirect, there are vast amounts of content. And this content is growing exponentially with the advent of digital recording and storage. The great variety, quality, and composition of data can be easily shaped to fit the methods we use for communication. And as we lead into the twenty-first century, more and better media and participation devices are offered.

CONCLUSION AND CODA

As teachers and students, we still face key questions about the intersection of content and process. The eternal problems of "how should I teach?" "what should I teach?" and "what's worth teaching?" must still be answered. These questions are basic to all actor/actress/teacher decision making in classrooms. The processes we adopt are critical to our success with students, much more so than the content. Why? Because the process dictates the selection, shaping, and editing of content to suit an audience.

Basic decisions, simple decisions, shape our performances as actresses and actors, as teachers, as parents, as leaders, and as followers. Coaches, bosses, politicians, citizens, families, and students all play the instructor role and the student role at different times and places, and make choices about curriculum (content) and delivery (process). From reading a bedtime story to presenting a formal public address, we have chosen a style of delivery and arranged the content for an effect. From family discussions of purchases to diplomatic negotiations for trade or treaties, we can play roles as authorities directly in control, or as diplomats sharing ideas to convince others to follow.

Choices about how to marry content with process *always* have a profound effect upon audiences. Even presenting data as neutral (usually a ruse of some kind) has consequences. Strong values and deep issues may sharpen interest and cultivate a taste for more participation. Very difficult, incomprehensible instruction can deepen feelings of inadequacy and lack of understanding that drive audiences away.

Therefore, our knowledge of methods and of materials, of data and technique, is critical to decision making in any instructional roles involving process and content, which are inseparable.

AN INTERVIEW ABOUT YOUR THINKING SO FAR: PROCESS AND CONTENT

1. Is providing content the most important teacher role?
2. Is providing skills the most important teacher role?
3. Is providing guidance and good values the most important role?
4. Can content be communicated without process, without a method, medium, or technique?
5. What do you see as the more difficult role, communicating content or process? Why?
6. Depending on your answers to 1, 2, and 3, how would a teacher best deliver content, skills, or values?

NOTES

1. Charles Dickens, *Hard Times* (New York: Penguin, 1854), 9.
2. Bruner (1996), 56–57.
3. Wilson, Shulman, and Richert (1987). This reminds us of the incredibly wide range of choices teachers have to make about curriculum and methods for all subjects.
4. A classic arguing, in a way, that process is the end-all and be-all for communication; yet here we are obsessed mostly with content in teaching!
5. Brophy (1996). The author reminds us that the audience is indeed a key to success.
6. Palmer (1993). This book is one of a relatively few thoughtful reminiscences on a teaching career, with suggestions for marrying content with process.

5

Cognition and Emotion

Being able to put aside one's self-centered focus and impulses has social benefits: it opens the way to empathy, to real listening, to taking another's perspective. Empathy, as we have seen, leads to caring, altruism, and compassion. Seeing things from another's perspective breaks down biased stereotypes, and so breeds tolerance and acceptance of differences. These capacities are ever more called on in our increasingly multicultural society, allowing people to live together in mutual respect and creating the possibility of productive public discourse. These are basic arts of democracy.

—Daniel Goleman, *Emotional Intelligence*[1]

In this chapter, my purpose is to draw distinctions and build relationships between cognition, or knowing, and emotion, or feeling, applying both ideas to the classroom life of a teacher. Usually presented as two distinct categories, these two vital dimensions of teaching should be thought of as closely intertwined and related rather than as sharply different categories.[2]

Ideas, for example, may be invested with considerable feeling, while feelings may indeed be formed from emotional experiences. It is for educational purposes, for teaching purposes, that we make distinctions. We must keep in mind that while distinctions may help our bookkeeping, they can also obscure our sense of audience-actress/actor relationships. Pure emotion and pure knowledge probably do not exist in separate realms but form part of a sliding scale.

From an instructional point of view, strict separation is impossible for a teacher of any level or subject. A totally factual lesson would render the instructor an automaton. A totally emotional lesson would

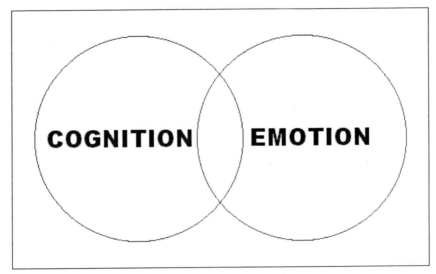

Figure 5.1.   The Intersection of Cognition and Emotion

exhaust the instructor. Most lessons are in between; but the big question is, what balance or combination would produce the most learning for an audience?

Cognition and emotion play integral and connected roles in the overall teaching process. However, although emotion can make or break a teacher playing his or her role, the lion's share of attention usually seems to go to cognition. Cognition may be roughly defined as encompassing a range of processes devoted to building knowledge, understanding, application, and analysis in order to reach a synthesis and/or evaluation, usually focused on subject matter (Bloom 1956).

Emotion, or *affect*, can be defined as encompassing a range of feelings and beliefs aimed at deciding on the "likes and dislikes" of people and topics. Emotions can range from awareness, through opinions and attitudes, to lofty philosophical values, judgments, and rationales.[3]

Many other complex, hierarchical definitions exist of both cognition and emotion. These may be expressed in a variety of ways, but all deal with levels of quality and definition distinguishing between two domains, that of knowledge and that of feeling, teaching facts and teaching ethics.[4] (There is a third taxonomy of psychomotor skills that will be largely omitted from discussion.) The focus of this chapter will be on applying concepts of cognition and emotion to classroom performance and behavior.

Because Bloom and Krathwohl's work on cognitive objectives and affective objectives (the taxonomies) are so well known, we will use their terms to describe what is happening inside the "black boxes" of classrooms, that is, the minds of both actress/actors and audience. But we will not simply accept the lines drawn between thinking and feeling. Separating cognition and emotion for analytical purposes may be useful up to a point, but we may also want to think about how they combine as well. We need both feeling and knowledge to achieve a working balance in our daily lives as teachers.

THE COGNITIVE DOMAIN

In brief, the "cognitive domain" taxonomy of educational objectives sets up six categories and many subcategories, graduated and gradated from low to high, a condensation of which follows (Bloom 1956, 38–39):

1.0 Knowledge
    1.1 Knowledge of specifics
    1.2 Knowledge of ways and means of dealing with specifics
    1.3 Knowledge of universals and abstractions in a field
2.0 Comprehension
    2.1 Translation
    2.2 Interpretation
    2.3 Extrapolation
3.0 Application
4.0 Analysis
    4.1 Analysis of elements
    4.2 Analysis of relationships
    4.3 Analysis of organizational principles
5.0 Synthesis
    5.1 Production of a unique communication
    5.2 Production of a plan or proposed set of operations
    5.3 Derivation of a set of abstract relations
6.0 Evaluation
    6.1 Judgments in terms of internal evidence
    6.2 Judgments in terms of external criteria

The cognitive domain rises by requiring more complexity as well as a larger and better-digested knowledge base. There is a clear series of steps, from gathering knowledge to understanding, and on to analysis and synthesis. Looking at the categories, it is interesting that the authors view knowledge, facts, and so on as the lowest level in the system, remarking that "the knowledge category differs from the others in that remembering is the major psychological process involved here, while in the other categories the remembering is only one part of a much more complex process of relating, judging, and reorganizing" (Bloom 1956, 38–39).

"Knowledge," then, is the basic stuff that needs to be remembered in order to work with much more important, higher-level thinking processes. The data are simply a base, the lowest and least of six objectives! Bloom and company seem to be saying that what counts in cognition is how we use our basic knowledge, not simply its storage and retrieval. After knowledge comes understanding and application.

Application, oddly, is the only category not broken down into subheadings. Bloom and his colleagues view application as a more or less unitary process, on the part of the learners, of finding and testing examples. Evaluation and judgment constitute the highest level because these involve testing for consistency within data and setting up standards for decision making.

How any cognitive process can take place represents the way the taxonomies are defined, consisting of two separate domains. Nevertheless, both cognitive and affective systems value higher-level reasoning over simple recall, pulling together ideas, and rendering judgments. Bloom and colleagues see "facts" as exercising mainly a recall process, as nonintellectual. This is an interesting intellectual distinction considering that most teachers, living and dead, have spent far more of their time stuffing in knowledge and criticizing students for what they do *not* know, rather than complimenting them for what they do know or the insights they share. Five-sixths of the taxonomic objectives are intellectual and call for thoughtfulness. Only one-sixth are collection oriented; yet much of teaching still focuses on attaining objectives in a single, low category of knowledge.

THE AFFECTIVE DOMAIN

A condensed version of the five-category "affective domain" for educational objectives provides a second dimension for teaching, and is presented below (Krathwohl, Bloom, and Masia 1964):

1.0 Receiving (attending)
    1.1 Awareness
    1.2 Willingness to receive
    1.3 Controlled or selected attention
2.0 Responding
    2.1 Acquiescence in responding
    2.2 Willingness to receive
    2.3 Satisfaction in response

3.0 Valuing
  3.1 Acceptance of a value
  3.2 Preference for a value
  3.3 Commitment (conviction)
4.0 Organization
  4.1 Conceptualization of a value
  4.2 Organization of a value system
5.0 Characterization by a value or value complex
  5.1 Generalized set
  5.2 Characterization

Basic to the affective domain is the audience's level of attention and response. In effect, if you don't have anybody's attention, then the act of teaching is probably going to be futile. This ties in very well with the notion that there can be no teaching without an audience, even if that consists of the teacher alone. An audience of one's self can be quite engaging, and offers few control problems!

Attention and engagement, or willingness to receive, are the building blocks in the psychology of learning. Motivation is a key to proceeding to higher and more complex affective levels. There is a range, from valuing, through expressing beliefs and attitudes and opting for a "commitment," to gathering values together in a "system." Finally, a life philosophy or worldview is constructed, and a "characterization" to guide decisions is developed.

The cognitive and affective dimensions work together closely, in harmony. For example, recall of knowledge implies that the student is receiving and absorbing data. Comprehension or understanding of knowledge leads to a willingness to answer questions, to respond, demonstrating a grasp of the information. Examples are asked for—the application process—and audience members volunteer memories of experiences and events.

Conceptualization of values matches the processes of reasoning and synthesizing because emotion and cognition work in tandem. Ideas are organized and analyzed (synthesis), to develop hypotheses and theories.

Lastly, at the highest level comes evaluation (judgment), drawing together data, definitions, understanding, reasons, and theories into a coherent whole, a gestalt! Thus, what Bloom and Krathwohl call a "characterization" is created and refined into a philosophical worldview. This overview takes in both knowledge and affect, theory and practice, synthesizing a model to guide at all lower levels of thinking and feeling, cognition and emotion (Anderson 1981).

Let us distinguish between cognition and emotion. Cognition *mainly* focuses on achieving knowledge and reasoning goals, whereas emotion is *mainly* focused on achieving goals of attention, appreciation, and ethical or value issues. In language, we often use metaphors for what we know and how we feel about it. We use words like *know*, *think*, *remember*, and *reason* for the cognitive side, but use *like*, *should*, *prefer*, and *policy* for the affective side.

In teaching, we walk a tightrope between cognition and emotion, tiptoeing across on a very thin strand.[5] We mix metaphors in our language as well, for example, "I'd like to know," "I want to learn," or "I hate mathematics." Thinking matters. Feeling matters. They work together in tandem. A teacher who is highly skilled aims for a balance between the two (the tightrope act) to build a powerful impression on student learning. Therefore we may distinguish processes of thinking and feeling; but remember that most teaching presents a mix or merging, rather than clear polar opposites.

SITUATED EMOTION

Any topic taught must be "situated" in a context that strongly influences both what is presented and how we feel about it. Feelings may be public and open, or they may be subliminal and covert. In many situations, definitely including classrooms, homes, sports, and business, emotions rather than cognitions are often keys to achieving goals.

Each person in the actress/actor/teacher role projects a persona and a value system, which pervade the entire community, producing a distinctive "classroom atmosphere." This atmosphere may be punitive or rewarding, controlling or laissez-faire, lackadaisical or driven, nerve-wracking or heartwarming. The audience usually knows and feels this atmosphere more than the actress/actor. Participants act accordingly, becoming talkative or silent, excited or bored, active or passive, in line with the tone set by the teacher.

In some fields, such as science and mathematics, many teachers may reject or be mistrustful of the role of emotion in their communities. They see emotion as the opposite of the reasoning and research required by their subjects. Values and decision making are seen as confusing, or a diversion from the overall didactic goals of the lessons, units, and course.

In other fields, such as social studies and language arts, debate and decision making are officially sanctioned as part of citizenship and culture. However, emotions can also be viewed as dangerous and problematical, particularly if these feelings go against established norms and interpretations. For instance, if antigovernment ideas and positions are expressed, many will back away from the discussion.

Emotions may be mistrusted rather than used, and may not be viewed as part of a situation and context conducive to participation. But the emotions are still there, developing as the cognitive messages proceed. No matter how hard teachers try to be neutral, feelings strongly influence judgments about instructional quality and the viability of content.[6]

Challenge yourself as an observer and action researcher. Acting as a student or teacher, search for a presentation of any sort that is devoid of emotion or cognition. The long-running argument about teaching skills and values independently of subject matter is amusing, since the skills or values are often embedded in a subject. Thus, emotion and cognition are part and parcel, integral and interconnected, of every teaching/learning situation. Even learning computer skills or driver training requires emotional ploys to sustain interest and heighten awareness. Even machines (which are, after all, us in disguise) need to employ instructional devices to capture their audience's attention.

So let's have the programmer appeal to our feelings and values. We need to have Big Bird and Oscar the Grouch pop up on our screens to teach us math. If we are still bored, let's play a war game. POW!

AUDIENCE PARTICIPATION

Write a 250-word presentation on a mathematical topic, or a historical period, or an ecological crisis. Your essay must be completely free of bias or viewpoint. Exclude any expression of emotion or philosophical commitment. Make sure your presentation is neutral and avoids any words, phrases, or expressions that are "hot" or "cold," positive or negative. Read over and review your presentation. Practice in front of a mirror to make sure you adopt the necessary deadpan style needed for total neutrality. OK? Are you satisfied that you have achieved the goal? Why or why not?

THE ROLE OF EMOTION

The role of emotion in teaching and learning receives relatively modest attention compared with cognition. Those in the teacher's role, including parents, coaches, film directors, legislators, and army commanders, for example, often deliver information and messages to those in the student/audience role matter-of-factly, as neutral communication.

But, as those of us who have played student roles know, there is always a tone or mood projected. An undercurrent, an ethical perspective or a value and belief system, is buried in that monotone delivery of data. In situations that demonstrate "neutral" delivery, perhaps we might be more suspicious about the teacher's purpose. Perhaps the teacher is, after all, simply conveying the information we need to us. Perhaps the teacher is himself or herself naive, or insensitive to the underlying message in the material.

In a first case, it is almost impossible to present any lecture, unit, subject, format, or set of data unedited and without a message. Striving after objectivity tends to produce presentations and deliveries that we see as boring. Dullness lowers motivation to pay attention and study, to interact with others in the situation, to keep on task.

A second case may involve a delivery of content so strongly shaped by ideological and/or affective goals that the information is almost lost in a wave of feeling. For example, discussions of American history may be presented in such a positive (or negative) nationalistic manner that any critical remarks are clearly unwelcome. The teacher seeks a patriotic sharing of feeling rather than any sort of serious conversation about political attitudes and behavior.

This type of lesson is a kind of propaganda, although it may very well generate a lot of positive or negative attitudes within an audience, and adulation or hatred for the teacher. But cognitive processes are pretty much lost in the sense of critical thinking, except at the lowest levels. Higher levels of affective objectives are not necessarily attained either. Affect, emotion, is used in this type of situation to promote an ideological commitment. Little is allowed in the way of higher-level thinking or feeling; thus, the performance tends to enforce authority rather than democratic principles.

The whole notion that teachers can easily separate knowledge goals and objectives from affective goals and objectives should be questioned (Goldie 2000). Traditionally, we try to distinguish between the two dimensions; but in actual performance, have you have ever seen a classroom totally devoid of emotion, or of cognition?

Human beings generally find avoiding emotions and judgments difficult. Bias and prejudice, tastes and preferences seep into every single lesson presented, however seemingly objective the subject. Emotions, drama, and moral questions add an advantage or disadvantage in communicating with an audience and holding their attention and interest. Sparking discussion and strong feeling is an advantage. Shaping opinions and attitudes can be all too easy, but it backfires when audiences feel they have been manipulated.

While we may have engaged our audience through using strong emotional messages, we may have also destroyed the possibility of "testimonial reading." This kind of reading is an egalitarian sharing of news and views by teachers and students (Boler 1999). If emotion or affect is too powerful, then the development of cognitive understanding may be overwhelmed by the flow of affect. On the other hand, we don't want to perform in a way that is so relentlessly neutral that the audience is bored or goes to sleep entirely. Teacher roles need balance, but that can be difficult to achieve.

Presentations of content incorporate decisions about quantity, quality, message, and meaning for any subject. Even those priding themselves on scientific rigor, as in fields such as mathematics or physics, are making selections and judgments. Teachers are consciously or unconsciously building preferences into every lesson in choosing and presenting material.

Goals and objectives set by teachers are also shaped by systems of rewards and punishments, which create a community atmosphere that leads to expectations for educational standards. Therefore, teachers should plan to use emotion, approval, and criticism in communications with audiences, just as we plan for knowledge goals. Planning would make conscious and transparent the role of emotion in developing student cognition, since reasoning and values, information and emotion, work together to promote learning.

LEVELS OF EMOTION AND AFFECT

Remember that emotions can be thought of as a whole *range* of feeling, from awareness to opinions and attitudes, on up to ethical stands and defenses. Just as cognition is conceptualized in terms of a cognitive domain, beginning with a knowledge base and ending with the processes of synthesis and evaluation, affect can be conceptualized in terms of another dimension, the affective domain, which begins with awareness, likes and dislikes, and opinions, and ends with values and philosophies.

How the two domains relate and work together in a setting and situation needs development, as these relationships are not clearly spelled out in descriptions of the two systems, which seem to overlap a bit. Even while the authors are struggling to make the separations as clear and distinct as possible in terms of setting educational objectives, crossovers suggest themselves. Building categories that are sharp and distinct is difficult, and they may not reflect the integrated reality of complex roles.[7]

For example, the atom is presented in a time-honored science lesson aimed at young people, in which there are protons, electrons, and neutrons swirling in lovely order around the nucleus, each obeying neat and clean mathematical rules. And each forms a mathematically perfect spiral orbiting around a center. This lesson is a simplification of "reality" by physics, chemistry, and science teachers for an audience that is assumed to need easy visuals, preferably in neat trilogies.

In actuality, the atom is very complex, with dozens of particles swirling around inside and outside, some of whose functions we still do not fully understand. I personally like quarks and neutrinos, much preferring them, whatever they are, to boring protons and neutrons. This rather standard science lesson has been repeated by millions of students acting as droning automatons, little understanding the complexity and beauty of physics, simply memorizing the material so they can pass the test.

Their emotions tell them they loathe the topic and feel very inadequate to it, with the nasty implication that the fault lies with the learner or the subject and not the teacher. Along comes a brilliant teacher, sensitive to his or her audience, who devises a demonstration of atomic particles using dozens of balls of varying sizes and trajectories, set in motion around a nucleus. As these balls bounce all over a room, or a table, students may show interest in the subject. The dramatic nature of the presentation provides a metaphor for atomic interactions, and a simile for interactions with an audience as well.

So why divide cognition from emotion at all? Why not view teaching as incorporating both elements as part of its own atomic structure, to use this analogy? Why not look at these goals and processes as interlocking and interconnected and overlapping, as integral to the situation and subject? Why not forget about the strict division of categories and look for commonalities, interconnections, and supports for the teaching/learning process?

Emotion in some shading or expression is part and parcel of a lesson, a unit, and a subject. Presented by a teacher, whether live or recorded, on the Internet or on tape, all subjects project at least hints of emotion and values. Emotion lends interest and draws attention to a lesson and indeed drives the lesson forward, as cognition alone is insufficient. Students, the audience, do not usually become excited unless there is an engaging idea or provocative presentation.

The teacher must also use emotion, or affect, to achieve a certain degree of drama. Without drama, without opinions, without judgments, there can be little or no attraction to material. Engagement and provocation both necessitate the employment of emotion in the total delivery package. Feelings come through the use of humor or personal reflection, or through a sharing of attitudes, opinions, and ethical, moral, and value positions.

Particularly in this day and age, with the Internet, videos, and CD-ROMs, the teacher as transmitter of knowledge alone can and maybe should be replaced by a nice piece of technology. Dry-as-dust lectures that go on and on for hours, relegating questions to the end (if then) and repeating content from a text, could just as easily be distributed to an audience via e-mail. Why attend a live lecture if it is exactly like a recording?

By the way, even recordings, texts, programs, websites, and so on are the products of writers teaching more than just knowledge. All include emotional judgments in some form. All have to decide on a method of delivery. A basic problem is interactivity: how to offer the lessons in a way that encourages participation by the reader/viewer. Drama, a sense of feeling, is often designed through the use of talking cartoon characters, little computer figures, or powerful images set to music. Emotion is built into a presentation along with intellect, to enhance communication with an audience.

Cognition aims at promoting some form of knowledge and/or understanding on a largely intellectual level. In Bloom's (1956) taxonomy, the cognitive domain is broken down into six levels: (1) recall of facts, (2) comprehension, (3) application, (4) analysis, (5) synthesis, and (6) evaluation. The lowest level, recall, is portrayed mainly as a function of memory and not an intellectual process.

At the recall level, cognition is largely taken up with processing knowledge in the form of data. The highest level, judgment or evaluation, borders on the affective because it is defined as decision making, taking a stand or making a choice based on criteria. A choice requires judgment, a sense of likes and dislikes, which is scaffolded at a very high level in the cognitive domain: "judgments about the value of material and methods for given purposes" (Bloom 1956, 207). Affective learning is defined as emotion largely taken up with processing feelings, opinions, commitments, and assessments.

Emotions cover a wide range of events in teaching, from the purposeful injection of humor into a talk to the subtle interplay of expression and body language during a heated debate. Affect, feeling, attitude, and emotion play a vital role within a lesson, contributing to the context as a whole, turning it in a positive or negative direction.

CONTROL OF COGNITION

A major problem all teachers face is deciding what levels of understanding and affect they hope to achieve for their student audiences. We seek to inform and enlighten, stimulate and awaken, excite and engage, but the materials alone may not do the trick, so we turn to affective means to achieve our ends.

To most students, the teacher's performance is a whole; only later may they realize it was a sum of many parts and units: information, problem-solving, issues, and debates, many techniques and attitudes, all encapsulated in an actress/actor we call the teacher.

Affective or reflective, emotional or cognitive appeals may fall into several categories. First, an actor/teacher must set the tone or mood for the audience by building an atmosphere—the classroom or theater or home atmosphere for learning. This atmosphere lives in a didactic, reflective, and affective set of overlapping realms, with the teacher moving from one realm to another, depending upon the goals that were set and the reactions of the audience.[8]

Building an atmosphere is key to successful teaching since it will determine the audience's attitude as generally positive or negative. Rarely are audiences neutral about a teacher, and more rarely still does the mood change significantly after a lesson, unit, course, or communication takes hold. In plain language, once the students have a negative feeling about the teacher, life becomes a great deal harder, and discipline and retention, to say nothing of imagination and insight, may be affected.

THE ROLE OF COGNITION

Cognition, defined here as the process of gathering, analyzing, and synthesizing information, plays a key role in the relationship between actress/actor and audience (Anderson 1981). Cognition contributes to intellectual development through the collection and processing of data. Data, content, material, and subject matter can be processed at lower, middle, and high levels of thinking. Recall of facts is defined by Bloom (1956) as the lowest level, a nonintellectual category, one that demands memory, short- or long-run, and which can be aided by memory devices to assist the learner.

Cognition may also contribute to intellectual development when teachers use problem-solving approaches with their audiences, fostering and sustaining growth in skills and in using both general and particular investigative "tools." These tools, or ways of thinking, can be drawn from a wide variety of disciplines—scientific and mathematical, social-scientific and historical, and literary and aesthetic-critical, to name a few.

Problem solving, then, is a key element in teaching; but the kinds of problems selected can vary from low-level memory retrieval and "well-structured" problems on to higher-level, open-ended, "ill-structured" problems.[9] As star actress/actor, a teacher must decide what categories and levels of cognitive functioning he or she will aim at for the student audience.

POWER AND COGNITION

Cognition, composed mainly of memory, reasoning skills, and judgment, is part of every teaching/learning situation. Of vital importance is a teacher's priority, for example mainly imparting knowledge or primarily engaging in problem solving. Lessons may fall along a range of knowledge and skills. Suggested here are three levels, ranging from lower- to higher-order thinking:

1. Lower-order skills for improving the absorption, retention, and recall of information
2. Middle-level skills, such as application and analysis, centered on well-structured (easily solved) problems
3. Higher-level skills, such as synthesis and judgment, focused on ill-structured (difficult to solve) problems[10]

Which levels become the typical daily fare presented to and requested from your audience will be a key factor in creating an overall classroom atmosphere. Research shows that the atmosphere created by a teacher will tend to privilege direct or indirect instruction, and lower- or higher-level thinking processes, with significant consequences for audience learning (Doyle 1983). The quality of instruction will tend to rise or fall with a teacher's choice and understanding of the kinds of problems supplied to or accepted from student audiences.

A key dividing point lies between stressing the imparting of information and stressing problem-solving abilities. Your goals, and how they are carried out, will have a powerful effect on every aspect of instruction and learning (Glaser 1976). Further, problems can be well structured, clearly set up by a teacher for students to answer with only a modest amount of effort. Problems can also be ill-structured, set up to increase the intellectual effort needed for an answer or hypothesis (Simon 1967).

Answers will reflect the cognitive-process levels of the audience members. Some will respond with quick, easy, and clear answers, while others will give lengthy, analytical responses. An audience will quickly grasp what a teacher values most—knowledge to be memorized and repeated back, or intellectual problem-solving skills. It is rare that multiple goals can be balanced in a classroom so that students are challenged on many levels at once. This kind of differentiated instruction takes great skill and attention to feedback. Once an atmosphere is created, one major goal usually emerges as the controlling force in exchanges, although not necessarily to the exclusion of lesser objectives.

Data or information, ideas and analysis, criteria and judgments are almost continuously being fed into an audience. Media and technology can assist the teacher in presentations and settings through recordings, blackboard, CDs, YouTube, film, and other media technology. Cell phones can be used for instruction, turning what could be annoying technology to classroom use.

However, data may vary greatly in quality. From political propaganda to business pitches, from government slogans to advertising, the issue is whether students can distinguish between appeals and documented, scholarly analysis. Ideas can also vary from simple explanations to theories about cause and effect.

Judgments may also appear in the classroom, ranging from product reviews to political and theological philosophies. Reading, viewing, and listening can offer challenges to audiences unused to higher-order thinking. An audience may find fact and opinion conflated in their eyes. They may settle cheaply on a quick judgment without carefully delineated criteria. Teaching and learning are supposed to work together in building both value and cognitive levels, but this is quite difficult in most schools. Time pressures, curriculum overload, and test preparation often force attention to shift to the "bottom line" of knowledge.

Teachers suffer from limitations on time and quality when faced with the delivery of large amounts of information. Encouraging higher-order thinking and examination of values takes time (a lot of time), while the technologies and traditions of pedagogy make data input seem easier. As data in the broadest sense are pouring into an audience, they must use their cognitive abilities to process the content. And they must at some point render judgments about meaning and quality.

Large amounts of data may be overwhelming but present relatively little intellectual challenge to preconceived notions or values. However, ideas, arguments, and judgments require at least middling if not higher levels of comprehension and analysis compared with information. Problem-solving skills could and should come into play at the point of data overload, and take over as the dominant process.

For example, interpreting a famous work of art, such as *The Coronation of Napoleon in Notre-Dame* or *Washington Crossing the Delaware*, takes time. Teaching either painting as data about art styles or as indications of social change is basic knowledge, but is insufficient to reach higher-level thinking. Student audiences may accept the painting as authentically portraying Washington, although it was painted a hundred years later. Students may accept Napoleon's status without understanding the symbols of Rome, empire, and royalty that enrich the complex artwork. In short, knowing how to read visuals is, in the long run, probably more important than absorbing facts about art that are likely to be forgotten.

Interpretations and arguments are signs of higher-order thinking and involve many levels of cognition, from supporting data to final positions. A really finely developed argument or interpretation must draw upon nearly all levels as it works its way up both the cognitive and the emotional taxonomies. If most members of an audience can express an interpretation and/or argument, that is a signal to the teacher that a great deal of progress has been made on a topic.

An audience must try to follow an argument, making sense of its form and organization, its central ideas and supporting evidence. They apply qualitative analysis to determine value, and make a decision or draw a conclusion.

Considerable skill is required to both project an argument and/or interpretation and follow it, even if it turns illogical. Arguments can range from clear to confusing and may be purposely misleading or very accurate. The information presented may be drawn all from one source or from different sources. Arguments and interpretations therefore demand a sense of quality and a grasp of problem-solving strategies, not just quantities of information. The same can be said for understanding definitions, applying big ideas, and drawing ideas together into a theory.

Except where an audience has memorized a fact, idea, or view-point, there is the question of meaning and comprehension. Giving data meaning and definition fosters an emotional state that gives audiences a feeling of value. Meaning integrates information into a student's repertory of knowledge and responses, and makes the student feel it was worth the work.

Problem solving is an arduous process demanding considerable skill and attention. It is not enough to provide information; audience and teacher must practice with it. They develop a thesis, a string of reasons, a defense, to marshal data as evidence. Meanwhile, others may criticize the data, reasoning, and judgments, pushing learners to defend views more carefully and forcefully. Audiences form a community for sharing and debating, improving opportunities for higher-level ideas and values.

As debate develops, cognitive processes speed up. Position taking and decision making become a natural way of life for members of the audience who are presenting their views. Cognitive processes shift more to the audience than to the actress/actor in this situation. In effect, the "students" are teaching each other and the teacher. The actress/actor/teacher has faded into the audience, becoming a student, taking a minor role as guide, discussion manager, and host. The former leader's viewpoint is one of many but no longer dominant. Power is diffused and distributed more democratically.

The classroom becomes a setting for intellectual and emotional development.[11] New criteria emerge, promoting the force of argument and the quality of judgment, the strength of primary and secondary evidence. Roles are more egalitarian because the cognition is being processed across a wide spectrum of participants. Tools of discussion expand, from debate to conversations among panelists or small, task-oriented groups. This process may form and reform many times, but the situation as a whole holds to a democratic sense of give-and-take among and between contributors.

Theoretically, in a well-distributed discussion, individuals join with others to form a social setting in which many views and free expression of ideas are socially accepted. The total situation favors cognitive processes that call for more and better data to support interpretations, theories, and positions (Resnick 1987). Members of the audience must convince others, and teachers, of the worth of their beliefs and views.

Problem-solving techniques may themselves be tested and criticized in terms of suitability and reliability. A strong consensus may develop within the group, or at the very least a sharing of the information, reasons, and beliefs that back up each individual's positions. Perceptions and understandings grow clearer as communication and explanation increase, and problem-solving strategies are applied. As ideas and strategies become more evenly distributed and participation burgeons, the audience and instructor(s) reach a key point. Audiences and actresses/actors balance each other, moving beyond the borders of their role classifications.

In this way, cognition contributes to a feeling of power and persuasion within members of the community of discourse (Lampert 2001). The actress/actor refrains from staking out a definitive position for others to follow. If students want to accept the actress's/actor's views, that is fine, because they decide to do this based on public reasons and criteria. This situation is a kind of power sharing among relative equals; each person is allowed to speak his or her own mind. Those playing the teacher role can invigorate the atmosphere by recognition and reward, fostering development of higher cognitive processes for as many members of the community as possible.

POWER AND EMOTION

Emotion, composed of feelings, opinions, and value positions, is also part of every teaching/learning situation. The components of emotion and valuation cover a wide swath of likes and dislikes. Tastes and preferences arise from background, upbringing, and personal considerations, and from well-organized ideological and philosophical worldviews.

Agendas, that is, value positions and preferences, ideologies and commitments, are almost constantly communicated to audiences by many media channels, from those that are live and personal to film, TV, and tube. Even the very youngest children display a surprisingly complex emotional ability, often finely nuanced and discriminating. Displaying emotion can be shaped to fit many circumstances and has an intellectual or cognitive component as well. Cognition and valuing usually work together, forming a communication link.

The affective domain is as finely gradated as the cognitive domain. The affective develops from a "willingness to receive," on up to a "characterization by a value or value complex." The highest levels of thinking and valuing evolve from teachers and students working together to use their knowledge and their values to form judgments, make decisions, and take action.

For teachers, this means that we can ask students, learners, to apply big ideas and deeply set values to a wide range of specific topics, problems, moral issues, and political decisions. The engine of emotion and the skills of cognition can be applied to any topic, thus successfully merging the two dimensions into the overall teaching/learning process (Jagla 1994).

A driving force in cognition, for example, is mastery of interpretation and position taking based mainly on processing data, ideas, and theories. These might be called "intellectual processes" since the greatest value is placed on mustering support for a point or stand. Reasoning based on data is the sine qua non of cognitive quality.[12]

But argument—defending viewpoints and taking stands on issues—also requires passion for an idea or value, and skill in persuading others to agree, change sides, or modify and reshape disagreements. Argument and debate therefore require a degree of emotion, an infusion of adrenaline into the presentation and position, but at a relatively high level of valuing (Forgas 1991).

The division between emotion and cognition in a classroom, and in real life for that matter, is by no means cut and dried, set apart in distinctly different realms of meaning and discourse. Rather, both teachers and students should employ emotion and values in cognitive, intellectual arguments. Conversely, arguments and beliefs can be infused with a degree of cognition, evidence, and reasoning. Neither cognition nor emotion stands alone, but the two may be made to work together as encouragements to engagement with a subject and as a way of sharing ideas.

Much depends, of course, on the quality of both the cognitive and the emotional input, stimulating value and reasoning responses. Poor information, poorly understood, is not going to produce a great deal of enlightenment, nor will punitive and negative attitudes. The combination of punitive communications with poor-quality information will inhibit any discussion. Why should a student respond to a teacher who has started off with inert material and then criticized the audience for inattention or lack of comprehension?

By contrast, well-prepared and interesting materials, combined with recognition for contributions to discussion, produce a most attractive synergy between cognition and emotion. In sum, cognition and emotion can be used to reinforce and motivate both teaching and learning in ways that promote self-esteem and engagement. Balancing the two dimensions takes an art and a science of instruction that privilege audience participation and response. A balanced lesson drawing upon emotion and cognition, in a mutually supportive atmosphere, produces heat and light in learning.

CREATING CLASSROOM ATMOSPHERE

Cognition and emotion combine powerfully in building a comprehensive classroom atmosphere (Tom 1984). Each and every classroom
represents a coalescence of factors, each important in its own way.
Factors contribute to an overall atmosphere that encourages sharing of
values and thinking out loud. For example, in an ideal world of "great"
teaching, the teacher, captain of the ship, is warm and friendly, caring
and thoughtful.

This actor exhibits a sunny disposition, draws students regularly
into conversations, and is personally interested in student views.
Our ideal provides a rich diet of interesting and varied materials for
learning, contributing to a positive learning atmosphere. If students
respond well to these positive behaviors, then the atmosphere will
improve even more. If the school authorities encourage and support
a teacher as they should, then this will be a great place to live in and
learn in. This will be a classroom of vibrancy and exchange, excitement and engagement. Caring will be a much-valued result.[13]

However, this idealized atmosphere is not easy to achieve. There
are numerous forces working against "easy" and quick success. Sometimes, teachers are working at cross-purposes to their own goals, or at
cross-purposes with the curriculum. Consider the many initiatives,
commands, requirements, pressures, rules, projects, and interactions
within groups that can detract from a central purpose, or distort the
best of intentions.

It is difficult to maintain a sunny disposition when the principal
picks on you for inadequate discipline, or for a lackluster lesson, or for
tardiness in completing a report. Further, students and their parents
may present problems. Some may apply too much pressure for their
children to achieve and complain loudly about low grades. Others may
never show up at parent-teacher conferences though they are the very
ones who need to demonstrate a show of emotional support for success.

Levels of disorganization or hostility are built into busy, frequently frustrating lives, and then redirected at the teacher. The
technology you want to use backfires on you that day, and your PowerPoint presentation may not work, spoiling your lesson. Your science
lesson on "What Is a Molecule?" may result in the feedback "Is it an
atom?"—indicating that your audience cannot define the idea you
taught yesterday.

A parent may express criticism and dissatisfaction regarding your
treatment of the little darling who is not doing the homework, the

class work, or the reading. Thus, you may finish your day discouraged and perhaps in a depressed state. Teacher "madness" may set in! Your emotional state, in short, may be less than perfect. You may have trouble projecting your sunny stage act to your student audience. You may feel no willingness to receive, much less examine and espouse, philosophical values.

But, as you are a true professional, you return to your philosophical principles and begin to rebuild the classroom atmosphere by resetting the emotional and intellectual scene. You revise your role and set up a new theatrical performance. You deliver a sense of encouragement, reward even mildly intelligent remarks, recognize contributions to discussion, reflect good feelings, and build student self-esteem. Then you select a few of the most well-tested curriculum materials, deciding to do role-playing, a mock historical drama, and a creative-writing activity based on time travel to a past era.

You seek to enliven students by drawing them into activities they will view as "fun" as well as work. Give out M&M's (for an elementary class) or carrot sticks and compliments (this is a secondary

---

AN INTERVIEW ABOUT YOUR THINKING SO FAR: COGNITION AND EMOTION

1. How is *cognition* defined?
2. How is *emotion* defined?
3. Do you agree or disagree with the way the taxonomies categorize higher and lower levels of thinking and valuing?
4. Is a balance between knowledge and emotion desirable in teaching? Why or why not?
5. Is it easy to use emotion in the classroom? Why or why not?
6. What are the advantages or disadvantages of gradating thinking and valuing into levels?
7. How does emotion interact with cognition in fostering student learning?
8. Is an emphasis on thinking skills and value judgments easy to achieve?
9. Can anyone play the teacher's role without emotion or valuing?
10. What kind of teacher do you want to be: Would you stress cognition or emotion, or strike a balance? Why?

class), or promises of higher grades (if a college class). Hope rises, sugar rushes, and engagement takes hold. Everyone is busy working, talking, and taking notes, and the classroom atmosphere is turning more and more positive.

A sense of madness lifts, and you take charge of your role again, renewed, successfully demonstrating the power of emotion wedded to the power of cognition. Not only have students gathered knowledge, they approach each other with a sense of "emotional intelligence."[14] They listen to each other and the teacher role-player, all playing intertwining roles. A winged angel representing the taxonomies of Benjamin Bloom hovers over your room holding the two domains, cognitive and affective, one in each hand, in symbolic recognition of your skillful application and combination of his principles to everyday instructional practice.

NOTES

1. Goleman (1995), 21.

2. Bloom (1956). This is the classic taxonomy that has generated decades of categorization, and that recent research demonstrates may have problems of definition. Even so, it continues to exert great influence and must be part of teacher learning in colleges of education.

3. Bellack et al. (1966). This was an attempt to offer an alternative schema to Bloom, but it never really took off.

4. Krathwohl, Bloom, and Masia (1964). The volume covers the affective half of the taxonomy (and there is a third on motor skills), but this has never gained the attention of the other two category systems.

5. Frank (1988). This offers a fine argument for connecting emotion with thinking. It's useful for considering daily instructional behavior and its effects on students.

6. Ben-Ze'ev (2000). Emotions are hard to hide in or out of classrooms, and this book demonstrates how powerfully we are influenced by our feelings.

7. Griffiths (1997). Perhaps some advice for Krathwohl and Bloom can be found here: Perhaps some of their categories are not distinct enough from each other, and perhaps some need rethinking.

8. Bernstein (2000). Emotion as well as discipline can control classrooms.

9. Frederiksen (1984). A somewhat dated but well-developed overview of cognitive theory applied to higher-order thinking.

10. Simon (1973). Teachers don't have to provide all the directions and answers for students: They need the challenge of ill- or unstructured problems.

11. Wellman (1990). This book describes the development of thought process from childhood, with clues to emotion's role.

12. Simon (2001). This is a combination of theory and practice with the deepest commitment to examining moral questions, dealing with the emotions generated by debating tough questions.

13. Katz, Noddings, and Strike (1993). This presents an argument for a curriculum of caring and justice: making emotion and moral values central to the instructional mission.

14. Goleman (1995). This book is worth reading on many levels because the author lays out a category scheme or ranking for sensitivity to others and for relationships between audiences and actors/actresses.

6

Theory and Practice

Every theory of teaching described in the literature is based on some conception of either learning or thinking and of the nature of knowledge . . . In order to form theoretical ideas such as those found in psychology and philosophy to a teaching operation, it is necessary to work out procedures and materials to bridge the gap between the theory and the practice. We cannot go directly from theories to practical applications, because there are particular problems that arise with respect to both materials and procedures.

—B. Othanel Smith, "Toward a Theory of Instruction"[1]

THEORETICAL GUIDES TO TEACHING

All teachers operate out of some kind of theory that is based on both psychology and philosophy (Schon 1983). Even teachers who claim they follow only "best practice" and do not trust theory are inheriting theories from their practice. Theory is inevitable because most practices were built out of more general ideas about how and why people teach and learn.

Even folklore and traditions draw from sources such as nationalism or religion.

Psychology supplies a largely research-based vision of learners. Insights into how the human mind remembers and processes knowledge, reasoning, and attitude is the realm of psychology (Cobb and Bowers 1999). Psychological theory gives us important guidelines: (1) the way memory works, (2) how people absorb information, (3) how people develop thinking skills, and (4) the role of attitude in promot-

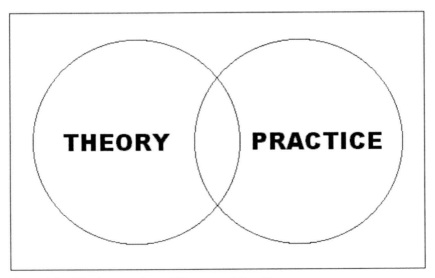

Figure 6.1.   The Intersection of Theory and Practice

ing or inhibiting educational goals. How we view people as learners is very strongly influenced by our understanding, as teachers/actors, of the psychological underpinnings of human behavior.

Psychology does not stand alone in education. The subject has been heavily influenced by philosophy. Many scholars and theorists influencing education have been both psychologists and social scientists. Setting up an overall view of teaching and learning is not an easy task. It requires thoughtful definitions of roles, which in turn yield clear procedures and a curriculum that can be defended reasonably.

Philosophy, the foundation of education, supplies a conceptual vision of knowledge and belief, guiding our thinking about what teaching should be all about. Whether to engage students as full partners or treat them as subjects is a deep philosophical issue. How to engage youth as full partners, if that is our choice, is a psychological question.

Philosophy helps us consider short- and long-term goals and objectives that should be a basis for sound educational practice, extending to pupils, teachers, parents, schools, and society. We begin to reflect upon just what sort of learning we want our children to gain and apply. Philosophy guides us to thinking about the methods appropriate to reach our objectives. Philosophy can assist us in linking goals and objectives to conceptions of knowledge, to assessing reasoning. And, ultimately, reflection helps us create a rationale for action, a theory of teaching and learning.

Bereft of a philosophy of education very little could be accomplished with any consistency or sense of direction. A teacher, a classroom, a school, a system: Each needs a vision, a mission, an overarching sense of purpose and role (Bruner 1990). In other words, the mission provides us with a sense of success. Very rare are schools or systems where all students meet or exceed standards, but the standards (if based on philosophic reflection) give us an ideal to seek.

Without a philosophy, what do we offer as ideals? Why are we teaching or learning anything if we don't have a rationale and a goal that are worthy of defense? How do we identify the direction we want to go in, and how do we know when we get there? We need both a view of human functioning and a sense of purpose. Ideals alert us to ways of understanding and setting a course of action throughout a course of study. With clear goals, whether for content or process or both, we can judge results.

In short, psychology guides us in understanding how people learn and how teachers develop effective practice. Philosophy guides us in offering a range of goals and methods for teaching and learning. We have choices to make about learning skills, content, and pedagogical methods, and these choices are guided and shaped by what we value and insights into strategies of implementation.

Taken together, philosophy and psychology offer theories to choose from for teaching roles and learning roles (Shulman 1986). Smith (1969) points out in our chapter epigraph that we need "bridges" between theory and practice. "Materials and procedures," content and process, act as crossovers that translate general ideas, like Gardner's multiple intelligences, into new classroom practices (Gardner 1985). Where we once taught some subjects almost entirely through language, based on Gardner's theory we will begin to experiment with visual and auditory stimuli. Whether the new theory helps us depends on our assessment of audience reactions.

Through practice, we test those theories to discover if they are effective with audiences. Each field has contributed to learning and teaching, one in its focus on memory, motivation, cognitive growth, and emotional life; the other in its focus on choosing goals and outcomes that reflect defensible rationales.

The subject matter and the way we present it, within the overall curriculum, form our communication channel to the student audience. The process of exchange can range from subtle to very bold and

---

AUDIENCE PARTICIPATION

When you watch a teacher in action (pick one, preferably in a subject you know), do you see evidence of the conscious use of psychology in getting ideas across? Do you notice any behaviors or expressions that represent a philosophy, a commitment to a particular method or style of presentation? Is the teacher consistent? Do the stated goals come through during the lesson? Is there an underlying agenda?

---

sends signs and signals about what is valued, what demands attention. Of course, the audience may not comply or may enthusiastically embrace the topic, serving as a test of both theory and practice.

Every communication has a purpose, with an underlying agenda, a text, and a subtext (Apple 1979). Sometimes the inadvertent or hidden meanings and messages can overwhelm the formal presentation. For example, using a social-studies textbook description of the often-reported nineteenth-century Indian custom of suttee, the burning of a wife on a husband's funeral pyre, may unduly bias students' opinions about Indian culture.

The underlying agenda distorts their view of a vast and complex society. If the description is based on accounts by only British observers, perhaps biased outsiders, we have presented a one-sided account with no Indian witnesses. A paean in English class to Joseph Conrad, while deserved, may not necessarily help students understand *Heart of Darkness* any better. Indeed, the glorification may worry them as they approach a "great" and difficult (to them) author.

Teachers have to be particularly careful of the feelings and attitudes they engender in students. They must study their own material and procedures from different angles, making educated predictions of effects on audiences. Otherwise, an audience may wander off, lose attention, or turn hostile and disruptive. Communication always operates on several levels, and in both directions.

While those acting as teachers convey more knowledge and attitude than is usually expected, student actors usually take in more than appears on the surface of the exchange.

A teacher needs to analyze practice as a means of understanding effects on students, intended and unintended. Students have a lot of time to watch their teacher, and many classmates with whom to share assessments. Those in the teacher role usually operate alone. Therefore, assessment grows out of a diagnosis of the results, as teaching and practice come together for audiences and actors/actresses.

THEORIES OF TEACHING: FUNCTION AND VARIETY

Theories of teaching come in a variety of sizes and shapes, all of them growing out of a *combination* of philosophy and psychology, with a good dose of experience and history as well (Leinhardt and Greeno 1986). Social-science research and biological research have also had strong influence on teaching practices. In the modern age in general there have been growing connections between and among the social sciences, the humanities, and biology.

Theories, therefore, are built and rebuilt from contributions by thinkers and researchers representing many different fields. Theories are more than simply explanations of outcomes. Each conception is an amalgam of great swaths of scholarship that cut across many disciplines. Lecture has a theory behind it going very far back into history, and much of that has to do with a view of teacher as savant, guru, and authority. Many views of teaching bear strikingly political and familial metaphors.

Theory predicts everyday performance, and demands allegiance to a specific set of rules and behaviors. A Socratic teacher questions, a pragmatic teacher reflects, a backward-design teacher plans and relates, and a Hobbesian teacher tells. Your conception of yourself as a teacher is drawn from theory: the ideals and practices that make for a consistent philosophy of instruction.

However, we are at a point in the history of our culture where many theories have been absorbed into a typical school and its curriculum. A portion of the significant ideas we draw upon work together well; others are antithetical or contradictory. Yet in a typical classroom, several influences may be at work hourly, daily, and yearly based on quite different views of teachers and learners. This kind of postmodernism, the fusion of multiple concepts into one stream of practice, is more or less standard. In a way, our heritage is enriching; in another way, it is confusing. Yet we must choose our roles no matter what, once we adopt the role of teacher or student.

None of the popular theories should be applauded or condemned; rather, these theories should be tested and admired. It is better to have a sense of direction in teaching and a working application of psychology than to follow a simple folk tradition or a set of goals handed down from above by impersonal government directive. The way to make a theory work is to practice daily with its goals and values, testing for results. Does this theory in practice yield the results we hope for, results that judge positive audience progress?

THEORY IN TEACHING: AN EXAMPLE FROM PSYCHOLOGY

Bruner (1969), Gardner (1983), and other psychologists share a view that humans have an abiding curiosity wired into their brains and minds. People respond very strongly and actively to presentations that emphasize problems, mysteries, unknowns, and uncertainties. Curiosity is aroused when confronting questions that do not have clear answers or that are subject to controversy. Mysteries are fun, in or out of classrooms, and most people are "hooked" by a good story. Students and teachers want to know the outcome. Curiosity, then, in psychological theory can be used as an engine for learning in classrooms. However, we enjoy these challenges only up to a point!

If the challenge is too difficult and disorienting, learners and mystery buffs may become frustrated and disengage from the task at hand. Yet, still curious, they are fascinated by the possibilities of new ideas and new discoveries, by the mystery inherent in the materials. Confusion and complexity can be exciting, but not if we feel lost as learners. Good detective procedures can help to allay anxieties, and this is where methods come in. We are caught between mysterious materials and methods of solution, data, and theory. Sherlock Holmes faces the same dilemmas: Facts must be added up to more than a whole, while he applies his own very insightful methods to solving the whodunit. In classrooms, this metaphor applies equally well to making sense of materials by an application of instructional principles.

We are a contradictory lot, since we seem to want knowledge served to us on a silver platter of easy understanding. Yet we rapidly become bored with too much of it over an extended period of time. Not only that, we ourselves, even playing the teacher role, want to be part of any investigation, to experience, if possible, the process of solution. Thus, we are caught up in a contradiction of control. There is tension between participation, active and authentic learning, and passive, spoon-fed direction and guidance, and there is tension between materials and procedures as we try to translate theory into practice.

This contradiction creates a push and pull between different schools of philosophy and psychology when applied to everyday teaching, as well as to administrative theory and practice. And there are very distinct "schools" or views on what education is all about (Kincheloe 2008)!

One theory of cognition suggests that curriculum ought to be posed in the form of problems, questions, and issues—certainly not as finished, settled answers. Settling problems and questions would, according to the theory, result in less learning because of declining motivation and loss of interest. If you choose to present materials as problem centered, then problem finding and problem solving will become a regular feature of classroom life.

Students, for instance, who hate mathematics have probably never experienced its mysteries. They are afraid of venturing into problems they have always found confusing, formulaic, and punishing. These learners need to be convinced that they can work out math problems successfully, restoring or building a sense of self-confidence. A mathematics teacher who can produce a sense of excitement and accomplishment, enjoyment and self-confidence, for "numbers-challenged" students is indeed a highly skilled treasure and should serve as a model for others.

Based on motivational theory, this math teacher would design mathematics lessons that made students feel welcomed into a process of exploration. Our creative teacher is seeking procedures and strategies, not just answers. Therefore this teacher may employ visual and hands-on experiments, building mathematical models out of straws or string to bring the ideas home. Each student would have a kit of materials to work with that exemplify but do not simply give away theory.

A teacher needs a way, a method, a strategy, for guiding a student audience to view mathematics through the prism of a psychology that values human curiosity. This is a psychology that promotes opportunities for exploration, even if failures occur. Failures as such are not punished but rather overlooked, to keep the motivation alive.

If participation lags and disappears, if students indicate they are waiting for the answers, then it is back to the drawing board to find a new way to link theory and practice for this math lesson. If students are immediately engaged and sustain an investigation on their own, then the teacher needs only a few well-chosen words of encouragement and the redirection of student ideas and questions.

Should you choose a philosophy and psychology that value the human intellect's capabilities for curiosity, then your teaching should call upon students to make use of their powers for inference and deduction. Then we must translate our choice into classroom materials and subject matter. And we need to decide to what degree the community can and should and will be brought into the planning process.

AUDIENCE PARTICIPATION

1. What teaching philosophy would you follow in the role of teacher?
2. What psychological principles do you think are most important in teaching roles?
3. Can you find examples where teachers use motivations to enhance student learning?
4. Which theories do you find interesting in teaching and learning?
5. Would you promote inquiry, or would you prefer lecturing?
6. Based on psychology, which teaching procedures hold more promise for classrooms?
7. Would any subject—math, science, English—be open to more than one theory for teaching? Would the theory cover choice of materials as well as methods?
8. How can theory and practice inform each other? Give examples.

Assuming we want to encourage a community of thinkers, then we need to help students develop their detective and conversational skills. Discussion and debate can be honed to a level where students guide their own studies in a direction our philosophy of education would judge desirable. Materials selected should support and encourage reasoning and problem solving by the student audience, through group work and research.

How do we know we are achieving our philosophical goals? By observing and diagnosing student behavior, and by listening to the audience evaluation of us, that is, of the teachers' behavior.

If students are engaged in lively debates and feel free or relatively free to express opinions and defend judgments, then we are most likely fulfilling our deeply held goals. This demonstrates students' confidence in their own abilities to work out problems and converse intelligently. We can reinforce performance by reassuring them that strategies are on track, useful, and valuable. This serves as proof that we are getting results from our role as motivator.

A choice of a psychological theory of curiosity closely matches and supports a philosophical choice in favor of reasoning and reflection as primary goals for teaching and learning. The two theories still need to be translated into practice by a judicious and shrewd choice of materials (curriculum) and methods (activities, questions, and strategies).

AUDIENCE PARTICIPATION

1. Do you have any theories you believe should guide your lesson planning in, say, social studies or science?
2. Would different rules apply than they did in mathematics, or is curiosity still a strong underlying goal and motivation?
3. Would you prefer a "stimulus-response" theory of teaching mathematics, one in which everything is organized around right and wrong answers, with rewards for the correct answers and criticism for the incorrect answers?
4. Or might you prefer a "discovery" theory of mathematics promoting student insight into ideas and principles from hands-on practice and problem solving?
5. Perhaps you would not want to subscribe 100 percent to either or any theory. Why?
6. Without a theory, could you be consistent as a teacher?

CONFLICTS AND CONTRADICTIONS

Conflicts and contradictions between theory and practice start when we as teachers try to combine priorities from different theories to inform everyday teaching. The results are often inconsistent. The whole idea of setting priorities is that *one* or *a few* ideas and goals take precedence over the rest. That is how a teacher sets a direction for students.

If there are many competing, and sometimes even contradictory, goals, then it is difficult to decide which are the priorities. The result of this is an all-too-typical effort to do as much as humanly possible for the audience from many theoretical points of view, often simultaneously. Sometimes multiple goals are observable in the same course, unit, or lesson. This fusion usually results in confusion and a lack of understanding of a teacher's rationale.

Pursuing many contradictory goals has the effect of washing out effects on student learning (Peterson and Clark 1978). It is hard to diagnose results from any one lesson, unit, or course if you change emphasis each day. This is the reason why considerable amounts of educational research on change in the classroom regress to the mean. Think about the effects of implementing into practice philosophies of education that simultaneously demand coverage and inquiry, or high scores on test of fact and elegantly reasoned arguments on essays. It is quite difficult to teach all knowledge and skills, reasoning and value judgment, all at the same time.

Consider your own daily, weekly, and monthly classroom practice. Or consider a teacher, coach, or leader you have the opportunity to observe on a regular basis. Examine the kinds of questions he or she asks. Zero in on what seem to be the overall objectives. Would you conclude that you as teacher, or a teacher you've observed, communicate a sense of consistency? Does the audience appear to grasp daily goals, as well as an overall sense of direction?

All big ideas, like theory, need a period of reflection and time for classroom trial. Rushing achievement or slavishly following a particular point of view without feedback from students is a risky business. Theory has to be slowly and carefully tried out in practice in such a way that teachers can reach a reasonable judgment of success or failure.

There are a number of popular and widespread theories that dominate most educational practice. Each theory promotes a philosophy and psychology of education. And each has a position on what should be part of the curriculum, the role teachers should play, and which goals give general purpose and meaning to schools. We might label these big ideas or theoretical models as (1) cultural transmission, (2) stimulus-response, (3) cognitive growth, and (4) resistance and critical-pedagogy.

Examples of theory are presented in a series of four sketches that should be taken as the briefest of introductions to complex and controversial ideas. For a much better grasp of the theories, readers must read one or more of the outstanding authors acting as spokespersons for one or another of the philosophies of education. Then you can judge which set of ideas has the best application to choosing teacher/actor/audience roles, and you can decide which suits your own style and preferences.

CULTURAL-TRANSMISSION MODEL

The first theory may be called the *cultural-transmission* model, which stresses the transfer of knowledge from past to present. In this view, enthusiastically presented by E. D. Hirsch (1987), cultures and ideas are passed or "transmitted" from expert to novice, from actor to audience.

The knowledge can be thought of as basic or "essential" content that should belong to any civilized and educated person in our society. These essential ideas form a foundation for our common culture, including language and literature, common metaphors, and symbol systems. In other words, we are taught a common culture we all share that enhances communication between educated citizens.

Subject matter covers both arts and sciences, as also shared in the curriculum. For example, transmitters would argue that everyone should know about the "glory of ancient Greece and Rome." Educated people should also understand the science of Newton and Einstein, the theorems of Descartes, speeches by Abraham Lincoln, writings of the Founding Fathers, and so on. They may connect with the Founding Mothers as well. These examples represent a type of classical education in which knowledgeable people grasp their culture's past.

Furthermore, they can apply knowledge intelligently, appropriately, and comfortably to many areas of everyday life, not only in school but when they grow up. School audiences growing up on a common culture are future participants in theater, art, science, and politics. In short, these are informed and interested citizens who support their culture in many aspects. Transmitters really understand the metaphors and similes embedded in communication, and advocate for what could be called an academic theory of education.

A philosophy and theory of teaching, of course, includes basics such as reading, writing, and arithmetic. However, transmission theory goes much farther and deeper than the information and skills. Proponents want to encompass those traditions, ideas, and values that are seen as contributing to landmarks of cultural heritage.

Transmitters privilege certain bodies of literature, art, music, science, history, language, and mathematics as central to a learner's upbringing. A shared curriculum is seen as necessary to development and as handing on important traditions. Sometimes the transmission model of teaching views students as participants in an acculturation and assimilation process. Essentialism means that students acquire basic skills along with the best classics. Classics are inherited from the past in all fields of endeavor, from mathematics and philosophy to history, art, and science.

Everyday practice that arises from this model prescribes a devotion to content more than process. Especially important is that body of content seen as basic and essential to cultural survival and job skills in our society. This is not to say that teachers are simply conduits and communicators of this body of knowledge, delivering it in a dry, pedantic way.

Many of the classicists, essentialists, and others who belong to this school of teaching want students to come to know and love classics. They want students to demonstrate scholarly and literary wit and wisdom in daily life and language as they develop into educated adults. Transmission theorists seek a society in which all have some stake in and real appreciation of the best traditions, materials, and works built into the school curriculum.

Many teachers go about transmitting works in their areas as efficiently as possible, but not very effectively. Often teachers assume that coverage and time are of the essence, and that as much as possible should be crammed into the average student. This stuffing in of knowledge, however valued and necessary, omits or disregards the underlying psychology of transmission. These are goals of knowledge: reverence for and enjoyment of the finer accomplishments of the culture.

Teaching enjoyment and understanding, rather than simply memory and repetition, is no easy matter if you are dealing with unmotivated or unprepared students. As the curriculum has grown and demands have increased on teachers, less attention is given to thorough consumption of classics or much of anything else. Teachers themselves may not have as good an understanding of the material as they should. Finally, as mass education has taken hold, a deep and thorough grasp of complex and demanding cultural traditions has become increasingly problematical to implement. Nevertheless, cultural transmission remains a vital force and lobby in setting roles for teachers and audiences.

SCIENTIFIC TEACHING/STIMULUS-RESPONSE MODEL

If cultural transmission is all about content, *stimulus-response theory* (or *operant conditioning*) is all about process.

This theory is based largely on the work of B. F. Skinner, who began his research on animals and ultimately expanded it to the realm of human behavior (Skinner 1948). The stimulus is whatever is to be learned—the alphabet, quantum physics, the vagaries of English grammar. The response is the "correct" answer, however you, as teacher, choose to define this. A correct or desired response is rewarded in some way. When a student responds in a way that is not "correct" (or at least not what you wanted), that reward is withheld.

Contrary to popular belief, Skinner's theory does not use reward and punishment equally to obtain desired results. Punishment is reserved for those rare cases when we want students to "unlearn" a certain behavior—what Skinner called *aversive conditioning*. Your job as a teacher is to reinforce desired behaviors so that they occur more frequently. As students learn how to respond to certain aspects of the subject (stimuli), rewards or reinforcements become less frequent until, finally, the students have learned what we wanted them to learn.

Although this may sound somewhat simpleminded at first, it can guide us, as teachers, to break our lesson, unit, or curriculum into manageable parts. The parts are communicated to students in small, graduated steps that they must master before moving on to the next level. Whether consciously or not, teachers reward students who respond exactly as we would like, and, unfortunately, punish those who move in the other direction! The majority of students respond well to a teacher's approval. The danger, of course, is that we place students in a position of saying what they think we want to hear. Teachers probably use operant conditioning on an almost daily basis, even if not deliberately. Who doesn't praise the student who participates and at least ignore, if not actively punish, the one who disrupts the class?

In a stimulus-response model teachers also come perilously close to a world in which there are "right" and "wrong" answers, and not much else. Transmission advocates argue that automatons are created who cannot think clearly for themselves. Sometimes, it is not always clear how a series of stimuli and responses should be scaffolded. In some subject areas, such as creative writing or art, judging results may be very difficult because of the huge variations in talent and individual skills.

Operant conditioning has trouble explaining leaps of induction and inference in which audience participants seem to achieve a "gestalt" or "aha!" of understanding that is more than the sum of the parts (in Gestalt psychology). Nevertheless, a stimulus-response model sets clear goals and assessments for teaching and learning, providing a compatible psychology and philosophy of education. Most teachers find stimulus or operant methods easy to implement for the vast majority of students, perhaps leading to better control than other models.

A COGNITIVE-GROWTH MODEL

This type of theory might be called a "developmental" approach because the focus is on the growth and maturation of learners. In this view, the development of the learner is the basis for choosing the methods and materials of instruction. Teaching is seen as promoting a cognitive-growth experience for students, replete with methods that encourage student exploration of knowledge through discovery, experimentation, and reflection (Duckworth 1987).

Student-initiated feedback and interaction are greatly valued in a developmental approach. Feedback guides our understanding of the levels of accomplishment that have been reached. The teacher is viewed as an artist and diagnostician more than a provider of information. Traditions may be honored, but cognitive growth demands that a teacher/scientist be keenly aware of student abilities and potential (Perrone 1989).

The central rationale underlying developmental theory is the improvement of motor, cognitive, and affective growth. Students should be enabled to draw inferences from data, form conclusions, and make decisions, reaching high levels of insight. In this theory, teachers facilitate development by providing a rich and rewarding environment. Whether at home, in the classroom, on the field, at a business, or in a cultural environment, those playing teachers build a setting that is both fascinating and enriching.

Students in this kind of environment are drawn willy-nilly into a learning experience and experiment. Cognitive-growth teachers offer powerful reinforcement for "inquiry" kinds of student behavior. Recognition and reward are given for the achievement of gestalts, "eurekas!" and "ahas!" In other words, a growth model places a premium on discovery procedures. Discovery in this sense may be viewed as an art and science of audience learning. Students, in this model, draw conclusions from raw data, experiment with hands-on materials, and build theory from direct experience with the arts and sciences.

Teachers arrange an environment that fosters growth, active and engaged, while posing thought-provoking questions. Actor/actress and audience work together to achieve a growth model, with more equal relationships than characterize either the transmission or stimulus models.

RESISTANCE AND CRITICAL PEDAGOGY

A variety of theories see the student, and not the teacher, as playing the active role in learning. In addition, resistance and critical-pedagogy theories present education as liberation from current mores and values. Inculcating revolutionary moral systems is the goal, rather than mastery of a certain body of knowledge. Help is offered in challenging domination, especially for those who have been disadvantaged.

Spokespersons for critical pedagogy share an assumption that education should not be intended to fit students to society. They see education as preparing and encouraging students to change society for the better. There is a broad range of those claiming to speak for resistance and critical pedagogy, but most share beliefs in the eradication of poverty and promoting political activism.

Foremost among educational philosophers of resistance was Paulo Freire (1970), who saw education as a revolutionary mission, one that would transform society. In *Pedagogy of the Oppressed*, Freire outlines his social and political agenda for schools to act as vanguards in building consciousness for the downtrodden, poor, and outcasts of the social order. His view of resistance seeks to overturn classical education in favor of a much more people-oriented rebellion against old values and mores. Education is a way of defeating apathy and speaking out against entrenched and unfair power (Freire 1998).

A more balanced approach to social change is represented by the "pragmatic" philosophy of John Dewey, still a major influence on American education (Dewey 1960). Dewey begins with an assumption that education can best be accomplished by using a student's own natural curiosity. This curiosity can be harnessed to promote open-minded discussion in a classroom where ideas matter. The teacher's role is to legitimize and reward independent thinking and reasoning. Dewey's philosophy is often called *pragmatism* because of its practical goals in creating active, caring citizens for democratic society. In this system, teachers play student-centered roles, and student participation is greatly valued.

As Dewey refined his theories over a long life, he began to see process as crucial to maturity and liberation. Learners develop critical-thinking skills that stand them in good stead over a lifetime of debate and decision making. Students assume a greater role in finding knowledge as a basis for defensible choices. A student who has learned to question and evaluate evidence as a step toward making a decision is a student equipped to become an active player in a democracy (Dewey 1916).

More recent theorists have played variations on the resistance theme, but within a common chord emphasizing taking stands on issues of the day. Audience/student roles become the center of learning, with the teacher as a guide or "agent provocateur." The classroom is a place of respect and cooperation, among students and between teachers and students. Finally, critical-pedagogy models focus on learning and teaching as liberating students intellectually and politically to challenge the status quo.

Critical-pedagogy models run counter to many current assumptions about the purpose of education as training students for success in the "workplace," as well-adjusted and quiet citizens. For teachers, this model requires a move outside the box of merely teaching a subject into the wider world of moral philosophy and political choices. It also requires a willingness to let go of "telling," to let the students contribute to policy, rules, and curriculum.

Pragmatism in particular seeks to teach the rules of democracy in a democratic classroom. Others seek to counter the system because they see little hope for a democratic classroom even in a democratic society. Looking at this group of theories as a whole, we find that open-minded thinking and social activism are among the most important goals, with knowledge in a supporting role.

AUDIENCE PARTICIPATION

1. Choose one author from each theoretic/philosophical model. Read each and take notes on the author's positions on curriculum, teacher role, methods of instruction, and school governance and administration.
2. Which goals and objectives seem most important to those speaking for transmission; for stimulus-response; for cognitive growth; for resistance and critical pedagogy? Why?
3. Whom do you agree or disagree with, and why?
4. Which of the theories do you think are most suitable as guides to all aspects of education?

CLASSROOM PRACTICE

Practice is the actual, observable behavior of teachers/actors in their parental, instructional, leadership, and coaching roles. This behavior is the visible expression of many factors. Each word, direction, question, emotion, and value grows out of a social context. One or more educational, philosophical, and psychological theories drive performance. Research studies may inform a teacher's choices, as well as reactions from an audience.

Practice may be based on a piecemeal approach to teaching and learning, or on a comprehensive, organized philosophical approach, expert or novice (Westerman 1991). There are long-standing traditions such as writing notes on the blackboard. (Now we have electronic boards of great sophistication, often with the very same notes as before!)

Taking notes dates back well into the eighteenth century and has been accepted into most cultures as standard teaching practice. Now we use paper, computers, and cell phones rather than slates. Of course, as with other pedagogical acts, what is written on the blackboard, slate, or electronic panel can vary greatly in style, intent, and quality.

The practice of note taking can reflect different teaching theories. Practices, though similar in appearance, may reveal competing goals and yield very different results. Much depends on why and how the notes were taken. Only upon careful analysis and inspection can we be sure what theoretic model (if any) is being expressed.

Novices, for example, tend to follow a piecemeal approach to the teaching role. A novice might employ one theory or model for one subject, and another for a different subject. As their sense of role develops they begin to work on developing a consistent overall style. New teachers, new to their roles, are trying out a variety of theories and strategies, activities and materials, often by trial and error.

As experience and experimentation accumulate, many employ the role with increasing consistency. It takes a considerable amount of time to absorb and integrate common practices into one's repertory. What seems suitable and effective to one teacher may not seem so to another. However, novices tend to follow expert teachers' practices, sometimes college educators' practices, in shaping their own styles. Over many years of successes and failures, they build a more consistent approach to subject and audience.

Expert teachers have tested theory against practice on many audiences, honing a sense of what works and what does not work. They connect content, theory, practice, and process into a fused method that can be characterized by a degree of philosophical and behavioral consistency. For example, "Ms. Smith" sees herself as a "constructivist" teacher of literature, meaning knowledge is interpreted and put together daily from sources that are checked and criticized collaboratively. Ms. Smith does not tell students what stories mean, but leads them to develop, share, and negotiate interpretations that are their own.

She has added a touch of "art" by developing a humorous, accepting, and easygoing style. This teacher exhibits positive control techniques, encouraging rather than dampening student participation and contribution to discussions. Though an engaged student audience may at times result in some confusion about answers and some misbehavior such as gossiping, the goals are involvement and vibrancy. Classroom practice includes teaching students to design as well as take tests stressing interpretive essays and document-based questions.

In contrast to Ms. Smith, "Mr. Jones," who also teaches English, holds to a philosophy where knowledge is either accurate or inaccurate. He is a thoroughgoing traditionalist who evaluates his students by how well they have absorbed the information provided. He has excellent and tight control, portraying himself as the authority in the classroom, both in terms of behavior and content. He enlivens and leavens this approach by giving a lot of individual attention to students, along with using his excellent storytelling skills. His students leave class with a clear idea of what a story means and have a settled set of notes for their next test.

Creating your own practice from theory is no easy matter for most teachers, or parents, or leaders, or coaches. Playing the teacher role involves considerable pressure to perform successfully with audiences and on examinations. Success is increasingly measured by tests and examinations that often place a premium on content and memorization. There are also well-developed, field-tested high tests of cognitive growth that measure understanding and synthesis of knowledge. However, competition to raise scores creates a situation in which practice downgrades creative thinking and reflection in favor of easily measured information bases.

Tests, too, are based on educational theory, but in practice they may stress content at the expense of skill development, or vice versa. Scores may be an accurate reflection of performance, but performance may be at best a very rough and inconsistent indicator of whether a student has mastery. As with teaching performance, a balance between lower- and higher-order thinking is important, but difficult to achieve in practice.

A major problem with designing practice as guided by theory is that established school traditions and directives interfere. Theories need room for interpretation, application, and assessment based on audience reaction and performance. However, schools are busy places with many competing goals and directives for teachers to implement. The result is usually an eclectic mix of ideas and practices that may work well with some audiences but confuse or repel others.

Worse yet for someone trying to follow a theory is the fact that those watching the show provide contradictory advice. There may be strong disagreements about practice and how to interpret outcomes, as well as about methods of teaching. Even the content itself may be in contention. One mathematics program is preferred over another for political rather than practical reasons. School leaders set up small communities that work well with others, but sharing across subject specialties disappears. All teachers are directed to use group work daily for all subjects. Results may be mixed, and a teacher's choice of style is inhibited.

As educational reforms aggressively try to reshape teacher practice, there are head-on collisions coming between local cultures and introduced changes. More and more practice is being dictated from above, sometimes for political reasons. At other times, there are genuine concerns about lack of progress, but the result is a "one size fits all" solution that produces teacher resentment. Some will view changes as impractical breaks with long-established, effective traditions, and others will see a cutting edge of educational change and progress.

Teachers have to defend their choice of role as best they can. Unfortunately, schools accept ideas and suggestions that compromise practice in ways that are politically sensible but educationally conflicted. These conflicts can involve issues as small (but sometimes important) as whether each lesson should have a specified aim that students can copy in their notes. In addition, there are arguments over terms. Shall we call aims "objectives," "purposes," or "goals"? Cooperative learning, group work, classroom settings, seating arrangements, school dress codes—all may become hot issues depending upon who, or what agency, is setting the overall philosophy of education.

Teachers, on the whole, would like to be able to set their own goals in their own way. Teachers would like to make their own judgments as to the methods and materials that they see as working for them in successful ways. Teacher autonomy and professionalism basically imply that the teacher is to be trusted with children and with the curriculum. The trend, however, seems to be toward the idea that teachers should be guided, tested, checked, supervised, and prodded to cover a prescribed set of materials using a specific methodology.

Somewhere between complete teacher autonomy and the demands of bureaucracy (local, state, or federal), there may be a happy medium. But that always seems difficult to achieve in the educational worlds where most of us play our roles. Deeply embedded into democratic culture is a preference for audience. Playing expert depends on the learners to a great extent, just as business depends on markets. If the shoppers don't buy, expertise ceases to count for much.

For example, even when teachers believe that higher-order thinking processes promote attention and interest among students, they

---

AUDIENCE PARTICIPATION

1. How would you balance teacher autonomy with educational demands?
2. How would you choose between teachers or administrations setting goals?
3. Where should classroom goals come from? What should be the role of the audience, the customers, in setting goals and standards?

---

may continue to bow to pressures for coverage and memorization so students can succeed on standardized tests. Teachers may know that some students learn reading skills best through whole-language methods and others through phonics approaches, but a school district may decide on a single policy.

NO VARIETY OR FEEDBACK, PLEASE, NOT EVEN FROM THOSE WITH EXPERIENCE AND EXPERTISE

In the past few decades, much has been made of what is termed "best practice" by teachers. *Best practice* is an idea usually defined as those daily techniques and strategies that seem to work well with most students. These methods and materials are then highly recommended for all teachers. Often, research has corroborated teachers' best practices, leading to dissemination by educators and government agencies. This is an excellent way to spread ideas and improve overall performance.

Though the "batting average" for a best practice may be high, it still may not work at every level or in every situation, setting, or context. Therefore, daily practice by teachers still needs field-testing with different kinds of audiences. And teachers need to study each best practice they adopt to find out what theory, philosophy, and psychology of education forms its base.

To sum up, classroom instructional practices are drawn from and must respond to a variety of sources and issues (Jones and Vesilind 1996). Among these are

1. Local traditions: the kind of support and the expectations regarding how a teacher is supposed to behave

2. Historical context: the kind of setting, community, and society in which instruction occurs
3. Audience: the group to which instruction is directed, their level, skills, background, interests, and motivation
4. Theories or ideas of instruction: concepts for presentation and subject matter, methods and materials
5. Knowledge of formal research findings: experimental evidence that an approach, method, technique, or behavior works better than another
6. Integrated, organized overview: a comprehensive instructional philosophy and distinctive, defensible style

PRACTICE AND THEORY INTERTWINED

Practice always takes place in a social setting or context, which may profoundly influence the exchange between teacher and student, actor and audience. First and foremost is the political and social nature of that context, that is, its level of support for and approval of free expression of ideas and theories of education.

How free teachers and students feel to ask and answer cognitive and emotional questions, provide honest and open judgments, and bring up provocative issues will have an enormous impact on practice. A community that supports the free exchange of ideas without recrimination will permit teachers to carry on discussions and debates in all domains/disciplines of learning. Students will feel comfortable expressing their views in a social-studies class, confessing their lack of understanding in a science class, and challenging a literary interpretation in a language-arts program—and feel encouraged to do so.

Exchange and sharing of views and theories of education will produce sharper and clearer understanding of goals and methods. Feedback will shape practice and theory. Innovations will develop and diffuse among and between teachers (Rogers 1995).

Freedom of expression will diminish in a social situation that demands or encourages conformity. A teacher who seeks academic freedom in such a community will have to fight to accomplish objectives drawn from a psychology or philosophy that the community finds inimical to their values.

For example, teachers playing roles that buck parental and administration pressures to raise grades must struggle with community ambitions that lead to grade inflation and a tendency to overvalue student accomplishments. Growth, teachers may argue, is best measured honestly and scientifically, so we really understand how the learners are situated.

Practice is also determined by audience characteristics and behaviors. Methods and materials, procedures and curriculum are strongly affected by audience needs and achievements. As a result, a teacher may decide to adopt a popular theory much in favor in the community or the wider world even though he or she sees it as questionable. A teacher may decide, based on experience, that the audience cannot experience success if that particular theory is followed. A teachers may also choose to define his or her role as one of stimulating resistance or revising the curriculum to emphasize cognitive growth, though this may prove unpopular with audience or community.

There are always tensions between theory and practice, as those in teaching and learning roles seek a satisfying balance. We seek a balance to achieve a practice informed by theories that improve student performance and growth, and raise important issues about which educational philosophy should guide us in the decades to come.

AN INTERVIEW ABOUT YOUR THINKING SO FAR: THEORY AND PRACTICE

1. How do you view theory as an influence on teaching?
2. Where do practices come from? How are they justified?
3. What is the relationship between theory and practice?
4. Can you have one dimension without the other? Why or why not?
5. What problems do teachers face in juggling theory and practice? How would audiences react to the different theories?
6. Which theory have you observed as most successfully translated into practice? Why was it successful?
7. How would you personally choose to implement a theory?
8. Would you expect instant success or a long period of experimentation?
9. What sort of audience, or community, would be most open to changes in practice? Why?

NOTE

1. Smith (1969), 108.

7

Teacher "Madness" and Its Causes

Madness, Euphoria, and Manic Depression in Teaching

I begin to see now. The logical order is taking a mental organization fit for grown-ups, chopping it into pieces, and giving
it a piece at a time to the child to learn. I suppose that the
idea is that when he gets all the separate pieces, he will then
have a whole. But isn't it absurd!

—William Heard Kilpatrick, *Foundations of Method*[1]

Civilization, in a general way, constitutes a milieu favorable
to the development of madness. If the progress of knowledge
dissipates error, it also has the effect of propagating a taste
and even a mania for study; the life of the library, abstract
speculations, the perpetual agitation of the mind without
the exercise of the body, can have the most disastrous effects
. . . the more abstract the knowledge becomes, the greater
the risk of madness.

—Michel Foucault, *Madness and Civilization*[2]

"Where do you come from?" said the Red Queen.
"And where are you going? Look up, speak nicely, and
don't twiddle your fingers all the time."
Alice attended to all these directions, and explained, as
well as she could, that she had lost her way.
"I don't know what you mean by *your* way," said the
Queen: "all ways about here belong to *me*—but why did you
come out here at all?" she added in a kinder tone.
"Curtsey while you are thinking what to say. It saves
time."

—Lewis Carroll, *Through the Looking Glass*[3]

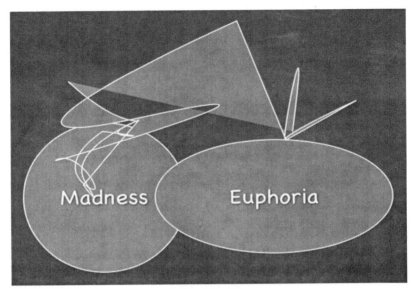

Figure 7.1.   The Intersection of Madness and Euphoria

"Madness" in teaching, as a classical and operatic metaphor, is very common. It is not a simple emotion, but rather a complex one with positive and negative characteristics, depression on the one side and euphoria on the other. Often, conditions conducive to "madness" may reach the clinical stage. Many teachers go home "mad" or "crazed" by the end of a week and are positively demented by the end of a term. There are a number of important sources of "madness."

While teacher "madness" may express itself as a kind of exhausted nervous breakdown, it may also be a form of catatonia, and result in the nearly complete cessation of the teaching process. This is exhibited as a combination of teacher manic depression and ritualistic role-play, with zombie-like presentations devoid of feeling—frequently increasing near the end of a marking period or shortly before holiday vacation or the semester's conclusion. A lack of knowledge or, even worse, the absence of student understanding and application of what has already been "taught," can produce great frustration for a teacher, setting the stage for what Foucault (1965) calls "the risk of madness."

There can also be an upside to madness, and that is *euphoria*, as we will call it in this chapter. Madness doesn't have to be a negative, and it may, indeed, be very helpful to a teacher conducting class in a less than satisfying administrative, social, and physical environment. Madness, or at the very least, the feeling of dislocation and disorientation, is very satisfying to many teachers, providing a relief from the pressures and stresses of dealing with so many people in a small environment, all of whom have requests, problems, and demands at virtually the same time.

The teacher, you see, is really a middleperson who is trying to achieve something while being set upon by the state, community, and local administration from above, students from below, and parents from the sidelines (Fried 1995). Sometimes there is a functioning union or association to fend off the forces conducive to "madness," and at other times this agency is itself compromised and put upon.

A "glass half-full" view of madness pertains to the manic, energized side, which can result in great energy, teacher euphoria, and a feeling that the students really "got it" and have exceeded reasonable and predictable achievement patterns. A good lesson with a lot of intelligent interaction and a high level of feedback demonstrates that students not only read the book or reading assigned but actually understood it! How much euphoria is experienced should be thought of as a batting average, and hitting .400 is awfully good, as the positive side of the ledger seems much more rare than the negative side—but maybe that is just because of exhaustion.

Euphoria, then, may be enhanced by a feeling of escape or of being overlooked by the administration and parents, and further fueled by fulsome praise for a job well done (which doesn't happen nearly often enough for most teachers, including me). Whether one wants to build a mood of euphoria also depends upon a teacher's philosophy of instruction, and whether you diagnostically recognize new learning when it happens!

There may be strong emotional satisfactions operating as well, with positive student feeling flowing to the teacher; reciprocal affection; a sense of enjoyment and play; and so forth (Felman 1995). Students, for example, may go so far as to request library time, in order to look up books they *want* to read because of your previous suggestions.

There is real interest in learning evinced as far as you can tell, and you are feeling that you really had an impact—that you got real results. Results seem widespread and solid, and you leave school that day with a sense of accomplishment. The feedback and feelings of the audience may induce a sense of euphoria for the teacher, and vice versa, resulting in what might be called a "positive" type of madness. A range of emotions may run across the more positive forms, from mania and compulsion to elation and euphoria.

Looking at the glass "half-empty," we can see the depressive side of instructional "madness" with feelings of being "let down."

These downside emotions happen frequently, on a small, personal scale; though the overall effect of a lesson may be quite uplifting and energizing to many students in the long run, this is not always immediately apparent to us as teachers. Sometimes depression and anger are felt on a large and impersonal scale, or they spread to a group as a whole.

The community itself may be consumed by internecine warfare, criticisms, petty jealousies, and struggles with and over students, resulting in what Thomas Hobbes would call a war of all against all competition. One might ask, in present "standards" parlance, just what metaphors from other walks of life work for education. Perhaps comparing education to business models is a fair metaphor, but our "product" seems rather uncertain, uneven, organic, and developmental.

For example, some students don't seem to have learned what you've taught. Nor have they learned what your predecessors taught. But we are not sure why there is such a poor effect. There is just a little bit of depression as a result. You teach the topic again, but they still don't seem to be able to remember it. Now there is a bit more of a negative feeling—it's a real downer. Audience understanding leaves much to be desired, and you become a little punitive. This is not a behavior you even approve of, but there you are.

Some want to leave the room for greener pastures such as the bathroom or lunchroom. Others are just plain obtuse and annoying, probably because they fought with one or more of their parents before leaving school, or because they see little or no intrinsic or extrinsic value in sitting in your classroom.

A few start a shouting match or wreck your lesson through joking and "acting out" behavior. Fortunately only a select subgroup may be "right in your face," talking back. This is not your fault, but society's probably; however, you feel the emotional brunt of that depression, and it may affect your overall attitude that day. So you leave school that afternoon feeling low, feeling that you did not accomplish your goals and your students didn't behave very well. You have experienced the negative side of madness, with a range of emotions running from depression to anxiety, frustration, and defeat.

Thus, "madness" is often balanced between its upside, euphoria and manic accomplishment, and its downside, anxiety and feelings of depression. Striking a balance between these two extensions of the continuum of madness can wear out a teacher, and is actually quite difficult to achieve in terms of keeping a positive attitude (Ashton and Webb 1986). Furthermore, your emotional state may be strongly influenced by other factors that impinge upon you in a typical school, such as your latest encounter with the administration and the behavior and demeanor of your audience.

Naturally, the more negative input you receive on a given day, the more you may be unable to hold onto your positive attitude; while the more positive input, the more your psyche may be bolstered and uplifted, and you may escape a sense of depression that day.

On any given day, there is probably a mixture of positive and negative events and behaviors, resulting in a mixed set of feelings, such that there is a balance approached and you miss that sense of "madness." A balance between positive and negative forces is what usually passes for "normal."

AUDIENCE PARTICIPATION

1. Why can't teachers even be totally happy after a "good" lesson, one they viewed as very effective for their audience?
2. Why can't a parent/teacher be totally happy when an explanation, set of directions, or agreement has been received, accepted, processed, and translated by a child/pupil into his or her own terms?
3. Why are teachers almost always dissatisfied and a bit "daft," as the English say, after instruction is over?

Let's take a look at the role of emotions, particularly frustration, depression, and anxiety, in the process of teaching.

FRUSTRATION

Frustration is perhaps the most common emotional aspect of madness in teaching. There are many reasons for this, and one of the most important is that teaching does not necessarily lead to learning. In other words, hard work, preparation, devotion to knowledge, and careful planning may simply not connect with an audience that is either unprepared or uninterested in the subject at hand. When students do not demonstrate audience appreciation and "learning," teachers become frustrated and sometimes even quite angry about the "failure" of their charges. When you have spent a long, long time preparing students, for example, to take their biology test, and someone asks you (again) the same repetitive question about the definition of *symbiosis*, you may become a bit testy. But you will answer (again) if you are a good trouper and a responsible teacher. Then comes the test, which this student and many others take, on which they receive low scores, lower than what's required for passing. Most have answered the question about symbiosis incorrectly, it turns out. A sense of frustration would be high, and might easily slip into an angry madness, with threats of punishments and torture in the form of more homework, makeups, extra test preparation, study hall, or notes to parents.

Providing these punishments might well lead to more frustrated thinking about why they failed. Was the material cogent, at their level, and interestingly presented? Is it the teacher, or is it the fault of students' lack of attention, inability to comprehend, or slovenly homework habits?

Maybe their home life is poor and unsupportive of academic success. Do you need to approach the parents to obtain their assistance in supporting their children to study regularly and critically? This type of fault-finding and self-incrimination produces more frustration for teachers, and thus forms a major component of what we might call, metaphorically speaking, "teacher madness" (Foucault 1965).

AUDIENCE PARTICIPATION

1. Have you ever been frustrated as a student? Parent? Learner? Lover? Teacher? Coach? Boss?
2. What do you see as the key factors that create a sense of frustration?
3. How could frustration be overcome so that we might move on to other, better goals?

DEPRESSION

A close relative and rich consequence of frustration is depression. Depression is a major component of "teacher madness," often evolving soon after the sense of frustration, when a teacher feels ineffective. Here you are, the power in the relationship, the leader, the fount of knowledge, the commander, the "socializer," and the guardian, and yet your child, audience, or group of students cannot seem to "get it" and understand what you are trying to teach them. Performances, knowledge, and skills—verbally, in writing, and on tests—do not measure up to your expectations.

These also do not meet local requirements, much less national standards of performance! This produces a lessening in your sense of self-confidence and worth as a teacher and results in a form of depression that can range from mild to severe, depending on how long you work with an audience from which you seem to obtain poor results.

Furthermore, you, as teacher, are not quite sure why the students cannot perform well. If they are rather quiet, and perhaps fearful of your wrath, they may not tell you why they are lacking understanding. Or they may not wish to divulge to you, a stranger, their inner feelings about you, your lessons, the subject matter, and the overall curriculum, toward which they may feel considerable apathy or even hostility.

Perhaps, you reflect, the students may simply lack the skills and background necessary to carry out their assignments at the required levels, and they may have been improperly placed in your care. Their previous assessments may have been misleading; or, even worse, maybe the members of the group have genetic, emotional, or learning disabilities that impair their achievements.

Maybe the students are recent immigrants and do not understand the language very well, and that is why they are doing so poorly. Perhaps you need to conduct a controlled diagnosis of what is happening and check students records to find out how many have poverty backgrounds, are learning impaired, are emotionally unstable, or require inclusion treatment.

Diagnostic problems, combined with lack of results, may result in teacher depression. You feel you are fighting a losing battle without knowing all of the key factors in your defeat. Some teachers/parents/ leaders relieve their feelings of depression by a kind of "reaction-formation" in which they do an about-face. Control issues become central (McNeil 1986).

Then those in teacher roles stop blaming themselves, or worrying about their inadequacies as teachers, and turn on the students as inadequate, lazy "good-for-nothings" with behavior problems. They thereby communicate to the audience their negative review of them, producing depression and "student madness." The teacher's rhetoric changes from one that is inward-seeking to one that is outward-seeking, from looking within themselves for answers to assigning or attributing causes "out there" to the audience population. Thus, the burdens of frustration and depression are shifted from teacher role to student role, but that does not necessarily solve the problem of "madness."

AUDIENCE PARTICIPATION

1. How often do you play teacher?
2. How does this feel emotionally?
3. How often do you experience feelings of madness?
4. Do you see these feelings as positive or negative?
5. Would you classify any of your feelings as mania, elation, or depression?
6. When you finish tutoring, parenting, teaching, coaching, and so on, what do you feel?
7. Would you prefer the student or teacher role in most situations? Why?

ANXIETY

A consequence of, or complement to, depression and frustration is anxiety. This is a third big factor in producing "teacher madness" because anxiety, or worries about student learning problems, about self-confidence, about lack of knowledge, and about social support, may make instructors nervous and alienate them from the very people they are supposed to be helping. When teachers are frustrated by lack of results, by misbehavior, or by poor achievement levels, they can become depressed but also anxious about how to handle the situation. The more uncertain they are about the causes for poor performances, the more anxiety they feel about future efforts.

Anxiety can be relieved, at least partially, by achieving a better diagnosis of learning problems and by sharing concerns about performance honestly with colleagues. Secret assessments by teachers of each other, by students to the administration, or of teachers or students by the administration may greatly intensify anxiousness and work to destroy the social bonds of a department or school (Jersild 1955).

More rules, planning, activities, and workshops are often the result of anxious teachers working in anxious school settings or more anxious parents working with children in anxious home settings. A well laid out calendar of activities produces a sense of predictability that is designed to allay anxieties about the future. Tests, units, curriculum, assignments, homework, reading, essay writing, and lunches have all been built into the daily, weekly, monthly, and yearly course of activities. Everyone will know what is expected of them and avoid feelings of anxiety, at least until deadlines approach. Then you can play catch-up!

Schools, homes, and businesses are usually very active social and political communities in which people interact frequently and spend a lot of time observing each other's behavior and listening to each other's language. Those in the teacher/leader roles and those in the student/learner/follower roles get to know each other quite well.

Through this community, learners share a great deal of communication and begin to understand how each member of the group feels about the problems they face. They also begin to see who does or does not support them in their efforts to reward, punish, direct, question, assign, and evaluate. Pressures tend to mount as goals must be reached—or, at least, images preserved—and team members, playing both teacher and learner roles, start to feel anxiety about how they are perceived and whether they will be successful. The administration, or whoever is in the role of "bosses," can strongly contribute to, or allay, anxiety by their own behavior.

A principal (derived from "prince of the realm") is the "captain" of the ship and has great power in setting the tone for a school's atmosphere, as either predominantly cooperative or predominantly competitive. A balanced approach is often difficult to achieve; but too much competition, or perhaps cooperation, can work to fracture, or bond, a community. Sometimes this acts so powerfully that either the group disintegrates into many pieces or unites into a whole.

The stated and unstated goals of teaching and learning become a kind of policy commitment, leading to expressions of agreement and loyalty (Lacey 1977). However, some of the goals may not be realistic for a particular audience, or some of the goals may be interpreted in such a way that the sense of commitment or loyalty is diminished or broken.

Because of chosen policies, criticisms, and personality characteristic, key persons in the teacher or student role may become disliked and will not be supported by others. This leads to more anxiety about their role and status, and perhaps to a deeper feeling of alienation and even worse results. Power issues develop, and unless some sort of accommodation is reached, these will fester and erode a school's sense of mission (Jackson 1968).

As you can see, teaching and learning have a great many built-in dilemmas and contradictions (Britzman 1991). These conflicts may contribute to teacher frustration, depression, and anxiety. Pressures may come from the student audience, parents, or administration, or the teachers. Conflicts may derive as much from clashing internal goals and attitudes as from exterior demands, requirements, and directives. Thus the many pressures, relationships, deadlines, and evaluations taking place in a setting may add up to greater anxiety and contribute to the overall sense of "madness."

MANIA

Mania is sometimes viewed negatively, as excessive attention to a subject, a sense of frenzy, with a person rushing around working quickly and excitedly, single-mindedly pursuing a goal. While this view may be generally accurate, it is in teaching that mania slips over into the positive side of the balance, into the glass half-full.

Teaching takes a lot of energy and a hyperawareness of details. It includes the task of simultaneously juggling curriculum, student personalities, colleagues, environment, and administrative rules and requirements. The manic side of human personality, expressed by a hardworking, hyperkinetic teacher, usually seems quite positive. Students feel they have the teacher's absolute attention and affection while he or she directs the study of a problem.

A passing observer, a connoisseur of teaching, may say this is an ideal lesson, very stimulating and effective. A casual and uninformed observer might think the teacher is "on speed" and dashing to and fro, asking dozens of questions, fielding comments, reworking groups, writing on the blackboard or whiteboard. This has a manic quality to it that most students usually see as positive and caring, if occasionally frightening.

Mania drives lessons forward; but this is just the positive side of the balance, and it may slip back into the negative side of madness if results are poor and the audience doesn't follow along and support the teacher. Acting in a manic way can be very productive for a teacher, but it is also quite exhausting and produces a collapse at some point. Collapses may lead to depression, particularly if one senses that one's best efforts to move an audience forward have failed. Then these and all the other buzzwords of successful pedagogy will sound hollow.

COMPULSION

Compulsion, a close cousin to mania, can work to drive a lesson or course forward. A feeling of compulsion is basically an intense commitment to achieving stated and/or unstated goals. There is a sense that the goals are so important to you that you are willing to push forward to achieve them, even in the face of lack of materials or recalcitrant students. A teacher exerts power at this point, no matter the obstacles.

Sometimes compulsive behavior develops when the goals are so important to you that you are willing to wear yourself out asking questions, giving directions, prodding responses, and arranging activities. You simply will not stop until most or all of the audience appears to have reached a level of understanding that you judge sufficient to meet your standards.

For example, let's say you are a social-studies teacher who is very preoccupied with the topic of the Holocaust, and you deeply believe that children should appreciate the complexity and the enormity of the problems and issues embedded in that historical event. To accomplish your goal, you create a PowerPoint presentation with strong images for starters, adding gripping and gruesome documents of the period that are readable and deeply affecting.

You plan several activities that bring home the sense of persecution and marginalization of persecuted Jews, Gypsies, socialists, and others. You press students to read and discuss the materials, drawing out emotions, comparing attitudes and interpretations, until nearly everyone in the class is exhausted but starkly aware of the nature of that tragedy.

You may come to the end of such a unit of study feeling exhausted, with the students feeling much the same way. Yet it is exhaustion from learning and emotion that most will not easily forget, and thus it is a positive experience. However, if the teacher comes on too strong to a biased audience, the results may be dissipated and the glass-half-empty syndrome will emerge. Compulsion, like mania, teeters at the edge, at the cusp between positive and negative. Balance has to be handled with great art to successfully stimulate learning and interest in a profound and touching subject (van Manen 1991; Davis, Sumara, and Luce-Kapler 2000).

ELATION

Elation is the beginning of euphoria, a feeling that you are really getting somewhere as a teacher. Your attitudes improve, and your emotions develop in a positive direction. You become humorous and cheerful with your student audience, helpful and sharing with your colleagues.

You are happy to be a teacher, and you sense that students are learning, understanding, applying, synthesizing, reflecting, and making decisions for their own reasons. The audience is moving up the scale of thinking and feeling, from the lower stages to the higher stages of thoughtfulness and reflection. This is exactly what you hoped to achieve, and you are becoming more excited and interested with each comment and interaction. With each informed answer and student-initiated question, you become euphoric.

Students are moving upward and onward into higher realms of thinking and reasoning, not simply repeating mechanically induced lists. They are expressing their own views and opinions knowledgeably, backing them up with reasons, evidence, and skills (Tharp and Gallimore 1988). You have tried to inculcate these ideas all semester, and now it is happening, really happening!

You are beginning to feel giddy with success, feeling that you are in tune with your audience and they with you, meeting in mutual reciprocity. For example, they are going so far as to invent their own mathematics problems, based on your earlier suggestions and preparation. They can solve them quickly and efficiently, and *explain* their answers to you and to classmates. Your giddiness is beginning to affect your inner-ear balance, and you have a sense of joy so intense that you feel dizzy. Thus, elation is giving way to euphoria, the height of positive madness in teaching. And you wish you had a recording of the conversation because it has the ring of Socratic truth to it, a rare event in an everyday subject.

However, compulsion may teeter over into mania and then exhaustion and then depression and then inaction. The line between euphoria and depression can be quite thin. That is one of the great dilemmas of deciding to play the teaching role rather than the student role. It is much nicer and safer and more enjoyable to be a student, particularly in an audience of quiet, respectful listeners who don't mind teacher control or even a bit of oppression.

EUPHORIA

Euphoria is a lovely ancient Greek term for reaching a pinnacle of joy, a sense of rapture. This derives from an understanding so deep that it makes you intensely happy and self-confident. This type of "divine madness" doesn't happen too often without the influence of Bacchus; but when it does, you suddenly have a feeling that it was all worth it.

Your endless preparation, invention, innovation, questioning, planning, goal writing, testing, and grading of papers has finally produced student accomplishment. You are Mr. Chips, a guru, Mother

Teresa, Socrates, and Confucius, all rolled into one. You see yourself as having such a skillful grip on methodology that you can teach anything to anyone in a meaningful way, if only given the opportunity. Your mania, compulsiveness, and elation have joined in a deep sense of having had an impact, a measurable impact, on an audience that you want to educate.

The principal or department head wanders in to watch the debate and finds it pleasing, noting your skill and your care for the students' opinions and feelings. This day your administrator leaves you with a sense of well-being and deserved praise. You take home their papers, which have been generally mediocre all term, and, lo and behold, you find that many have expressed themselves with what seems like genuine interest and feeling. Their reflections are based on the texts they have studied; they are quoting passages directly, paraphrasing intelligently, and polishing their assignments. Another piece of the puzzle comes together and leads you to believe that your strategy for presenting has power, so you save this as a valuable addition to your repertory of "great" lessons.

Euphoria arrives, built on a sense of powerful interaction between audience and actress/actor, plus a strong sense of connection between subject matter and thoughtfulness among students, with the added fillip of praise and recognition from colleagues and superiors for a job well done. You go home exhausted but feeling that you and this topic really got through to the students, and the glass is definitely more than half-full, not half-empty.

Yet, alas, lurking around the corner the next day is disappointment: Euphoria evaporates. Students seem to be apathetic about the new topic and worried about preparing for a forthcoming test. They bicker among themselves about gender and status relationships. You cannot repeat the last performance, and you give up trying.

Then you think to yourself that perhaps this is a natural cycle of rising and falling interest: that the audience cannot sustain deep and strong interest for more than a limited period of time, and they are resting in between high points. So you move on to reviewing for the test (boring, but acceptable to the audience). You try to deal with the gossips and the misdirected for that day, looking forward to a renewed sense of euphoria on another occasion.

The emotional dilemma of teaching and caring deeply provides the drive for euphoria and the warding off of madness. The highs and the lows of teaching are closely intertwined and are related to local situations. A host of players influence your attitudes, lessons, and overall sense of direction and self-worth. Although teachers try to regulate and control performance, set the rules, and plan the curriculum, outcomes can vary widely day by day.

Frustration can set in quickly; but in the hands of a dedicated role-player, this does not cause paralysis or defeat. Teachers can fight back by helping students "learn to transgress," that is, by helping them learn to become active advocates for their own needs and for social causes (hooks 1994).

Teaching is a complicated affair with its own emotional rules, even for those who have reduced themselves to a kind of automatic instructional plan. Even if you hew to textbooks, school curriculum guides, and state mandates with the expectation of distancing euphoria and depression, events may prove otherwise.

Any normal week of instruction can turn sour, in almost any setting: classroom, business office, university, theater, or playing field. Yet you apply theory to practice, and test practice against theory, and revise the content again. Choose a new approach, a more engaging one, and see if that works. Again you try as the teacher to revise and change roles so your audience awakens.

CONCLUSION AND CODA

Playing the role of teacher to an audience demands a peak performance that is cognitive and affective, intellectual and emotional (Sarason 1993). While many teachers try to focus on content—the subject matter as major goal—their personalities, feelings, attitudes, and moods cannot but interject themselves into the actress/actor-audience equation. This may tip the balance toward the positive or negative. It is awfully difficult to remain objective and neutral, to make a perfect prediction.

How many nations in the history of the world have predicted the future and gotten away with it? How many people have successfully maneuvered the shoals and reefs and currents of social life unscathed by alliances and feuds, family feelings and conflict? Therefore, teaching, being a social and communicative act, yields to social and emotional pressures. Classrooms are small societies, much like businesses, sports teams, acting companies, families, groups of friends, and political communities. There are always people acting and receiving, and sending feedback.

Striking a balance between euphoria and depression is difficult but worth the trial. Classrooms include a cast of characters worthy of a soap opera in a village setting, and there is no escape from the consequences. Effects can range widely from euphoria, elation, mania, and compulsion to anxiety and depression. As the emotions gather and peak, each of us in the teaching role comes closer to a form of "madness." This is a sense that it is all just too, too much to handle, and that we personally have "failed" to have any effect that we notice.

As teachers, we all need and want to take home with us a sense of self-worth and job satisfaction. But we sometimes underestimate the complexity of instruction and the problems of our audience. We do not take stock of the many roles we play, or the potential for new roles in creative combinations.

We often restrict our roles to traditional acts, putting aside all of the wonderful possibilities for expanding our repertory by reaching for a balance. We may play with art and science, content and process, but go no further. Emotion is avoided, only cognition sought, or we aim for practice without theory. Playing or stressing a few roles over many others deprives us of experimentation, and of diagnosis of student reactions to new ideas.

Refusing to change places with students and see the classroom from their viewpoint puts us at a disadvantage (Apple 1995). Seeing the world as our audience gives perspective and insight into the knowledge that they do or do not value, rightly or wrongly. Keeping track of student views gives us a marketing strategy. Teachers can develop much better practices if they understand student needs, interests, and deficiencies.

Expanding our roles will help all of us see the world of teaching and learning through the eyes of actors and audiences simultaneously (Bruner 1986). Playing out roles we have never really tried before expands our minds, our practice, and our stagecraft. This gives a shot at a few days of euphoria rather than a steady but dreary lifetime of instruction.

So, by all means, try out many new roles. Try these roles with all kinds of student audiences. Suggest roles to colleagues who have burned out. Take suggestions from colleagues, parents, students, and even administration for new and different roles. And, finally, try out all of the roles described in this book and decide for yourself which really contribute to the joy and euphoria and love of teaching, and which lead to frustration (Swidler 2001).

This book is designed to be analytical and suggestive—not to create perfection or terrific test results. It is offered to you as a stimulus toward thinking about (and repeatedly rethinking about) how teacher and student roles are played out. Role taking and role making, taken together, lie at the heart of all communication in teaching—in school or the home, at work or in business, or on the field. By choosing our roles with sensitivity and passion, we may prevail as teachers even in a bureaucratic and conformist environment.

**AN INTERVIEW ABOUT YOUR THINKING SO FAR:
MADNESS AND EUPHORIA**

1. Do you think teaching is an easy or difficult job? Why?
2. Which roles do you see as most effective with students?
3. Do any of the roles have less impact than others?
4. Do dilemmas and contradictions worry you, driving you to madness?
5. What kinds of student behaviors frustrate teachers, and what kinds elate teachers? Give examples.
6. Does going "on stage" to teach make you anxious each day? Each semester? When you have to work with new students?
7. How can anxieties and frustrations be overcome to achieve a modicum of balance? Could you provide a formula?
8. What would be the ideal classroom in order for you to feel euphoria? Explain.
9. Do you think each day will be perfect? Is that possible in teaching?
10. Can you develop a way to balance many different roles?
11. Which role not used or emphasized before would you most like to add to your repertory?

NOTES

1. Kilpatrick (1926), 304.
2. Foucault (1965), 217.
3. Lewis Carroll, *Through the Looking Glass*, in *The Annotated Alice* (New York: Bramhall House, 1960), 206.

Bibliography

Alexander, P. A., Fives, H., Buehl, M. M., and Mulhern, J. 2002. Teaching as persuasion. *Teaching and Teacher Education*, 18(7), 795–813.

Anderson, J. R. (ed.). 1981. *Cognitive skills and their acquisition*. Hillsdale, NJ: Erlbaum.

Apple, M. 1979. *Ideology and curriculum*. Routledge & Kegan Paul.

———. 1995. *Education and power*, 2nd ed. New York: Routledge.

Arrien, A. 1992. *Signs of life*. Sonoma, CA: Arcus.

Ashton, P. T., and Webb, R. B. 1986. *Making a difference: Teachers' sense of efficacy and student achievement*. White Plains, NY: Longman.

Augustine. 1938. *Concerning the teacher*. Trans. G. G. Leckie. New York: Appleton-Century-Crofts.

Bagley, W. C. 1908. *Classroom management*. New York: Macmillan.

Ball, D. L. 1992. Magical hopes: Manipulatives and the reform of mathematics education. *American Educator*, 16(2), 14–18, 46–47.

Barber, B. 1984. *Strong democracy*. Berkeley: University of California Press.

Bellack, A., Kliebard, H., Hyman, R., and Smith, F., Jr. 1966. *The language of the classroom*. New York: Teachers College Press.

Ben-Ze'ev, A. 2000. *The subtlety of emotions*. Cambridge, MA: MIT Press.

Berliner, D. C. 1983. Executive functions of teaching. *Instructor*, 43, 28–40.

Berliner, D., and Casanova, U. 1993. *Putting research to work in your school*. New York: Scholastic.

Bernstein, B. 2000. *Pedagogy, symbolic control, and identity: Theory, research, critique*, 2nd ed. New York: Rowman & Littlefield.

Bloom, B. S. (ed.). 1956. *Taxonomy of educational objectives: The classification of educational goals, handbook I; The cognitive domain*. New York: David McKay.

Blumenfeld, P. C., Hamilton, V. L., Bossert, S. T., Wessels, K., and Meece, J. 1983. Teacher talk and student talk: Socialization into the student role. In J. Levine and M. Wang (eds.), *Teacher and student perceptions: Implications for learning*, 143–92. Hillsdale, NJ: Erlbaum.

Boler, B. 1999. *Feeling power: Emotions and education*. New York: Routledge.

Britzman, D. 1991. *Practice makes practice: A critical study of learning to teach*. Albany: State University of New York Press.

Brophy, J. 1996. *Teaching problem students*. New York: Guilford.

Brown, A., Ash, D., Rutherford, M., Nagakawa, K., Gordon, A., and Campioine, J. L. 1993. Distributed expertise in the classroom. In G. Salomon (ed.), *Distributed cognitions: Psychological and educational considerations*, 188–228. Cambridge, UK: Cambridge University Press.

Brown, J. S., Collins, A., and Duguid, P. 1989. Situated cognition and the culture of learning. *Educational Researcher*, 18, 32–42.

Bruner, J. 1960. *The process of education*. Cambridge, MA: Harvard University Press.

———. 1986. *Actual minds, possible worlds*. Cambridge, MA: Harvard University Press.

———. 1990. *Acts of meaning*. Cambridge, MA: Harvard University Press.

———. 1996. *The culture of education*. Cambridge, MA: Harvard University Press.

Bruner, J. S. 1969. *On knowing: Essays for the left hand*. Cambridge, MA: Harvard University Press.

Butler, R., and Newman, O. 1995. Effects of task and ego achievement goals on help-seeking behaviors and attitudes. *Journal of Educational Psychology*, 87, 261–71.

Chazan, D., and Ball, D. 1995. *Beyond exhortations not to tell: The teacher's role in discussion-intensive pedagogy*. Research report 95. East Lansing: National Center for Teaching and Learning, Michigan State University.

Cherryholmes, C. 1988. *Power and criticism: Poststructural investigations in education*. New York: Teachers College Press.

Cobb, P., and Bowers, J. S. 1999. Cognitive and situated learning perspectives in theory and practice. *Educational Researcher*, 28(2), 4–15.

Cohen, D. K. 1989. Teaching practice: Plus ca change . . . In P. W. Jackson (ed.), *Contributing to educational change: Perspectives on research and practice*, 27–84. Berkeley: McCutcheon.

Cuban, L. 1984. *How teachers taught: Constancy and change in American classrooms*. New York: Longman.

Dalton, M. M. 2004. *The Hollywood curriculum: Teachers in the movies*. New York: Peter Lang.

Danielson, C. 1996. *Enhancing professional practice: A framework for teaching*. Alexandria, VA: Association for Supervision and Curriculum Development.

Davis, B., Sumara, D., and Luce-Kapler, R. 2000. *Engaging minds: Learning and teaching in a complex world*. Mahwah, NJ: Lawrence Erlbaum

Demetriou, A., Mouyi, A., and Spanoudis, G. 2010. The development of mental processing. In W. F. Overton (ed.), *Biology, cognition and methods across the lifespan*, 36–55. Hoboken, NJ: Wiley.

Dewey, J. 1911/1975. *Moral principles in education*. Carbondale, IL: Southern Illinois University Press.

——. 1915. *School and society.* Chicago: University of Chicago Press.

——. 1916. *Democracy and education: An introduction to the philosophy of education.* New York: Macmillan.

——. 1929. *The sources for a science of education.* New York: Horace Liveright.

——. 1960. *The child and the curriculum.* Chicago: University of Chicago Press.

——. 1998. *How we think.* Boston: Houghton Mifflin.

Dillon, J. T. 1988. *Questioning and teaching: A manual of practice.* New York: Teachers College Press.

Doyle, W. 1983. Academic work. *Review of Educational Research,* 53, 159–99.

Duckworth, E. 1987. *On the having of wonderful ideas.* New York: Teachers College Press.

Eble, K. 1988. *The craft of teaching,* 2nd ed. San Francisco: Jossey-Bass.

Egan, K. 1992. *Imagination in teaching and learning.* London: Routledge.

Eisner, E. 1993. The education of vision. *Educational Horizons,* 71(2), 80–85.

——. 1994. *The educational imagination: On the design and evaluation of school programs.* Upper Saddle River, NJ: Prentice-Hall.

Evans, D. 2001. *Emotion: The science of sentiment.* Oxford: Oxford University Press.

Felman, S. 1995. Education and crisis, or the vicissitudes of teaching. In C. Caruth (ed.), *Trauma: Explorations in memory,* 13–60. Baltimore: Johns Hopkins University Press.

Fenstermacher, G. 1990. The concepts of method and manner in teaching. In F. Oser, A. Dick, and J.-L. Patry (eds.), *Effective and responsible teaching: The new synthesis,* 95–108. San Francisco: Jossey-Bass.

Forgas, J. P. 1991. *Emotion and social judgments.* Oxford: Pergamon Press.

Foucault, M. 1965. *Madness and civilization: A history of insanity in the age of reason.* New York: Vintage Books.

——. 1995. *Discipline and punish.* New York: Vintage Books.

Frank, R. 1988. *Passions within reason: The strategic role of the emotions.* London: Norton.

Frederiksen, N. 1984. Implications of cognitive theory for instruction in problem solving. *Review of Educational Research,* 54(3), 363–403.

Freire, P. 1970. *Pedagogy of the oppressed.* Trans. B. Ramos. New York: Continuum.

——. 1972. *Pedagogy of the oppressed.* Trans. B. Ramos. New York: Seabury Press.

——. 1998. *Pedagogy and freedom: Ethics, democracy, and civic courage.* Lanham, MD: Rowman & Littlefield.

Fried, E. R. 1995. *The passionate teacher: A practical guide.* Boston: Beacon.

Gardner, H. 1983. *Frames of mind: The theory of multiple intelligences.* New York: Basic Books

——. 1985. *The mind's new science.* New York: Basic Books.

——. 1993. *Multiple intelligences: The theory in practice.* New York: Basic Books.

———. 1995. *A theory of multiple intelligences.* Cambridge, MA: Harvard University Press.

Glaser, R. 1976. Cognitive psychology and instructional design. In D. Klahr (ed.), *Cognition and instruction.* Hillsdale, NJ: Erlbaum.

Goldie, P. 2000. *The emotions: A philosophical exploration.* Oxford: Oxford University Press.

Goldstein, M., and Michaels, C. 1985. *Empathy: Developmental training and consequences.* Hillsdale, NJ: Erlbaum.

Goleman, D. 1995. *Emotional intelligence.* New York: Bantam Books.

Grasha, T. 1996. *Teaching with style.* Pittsburgh: Alliance Publishers.

Greene, M. 1978. *Teacher as stranger: Educational philosophy for the modern age.* Belmont, CA: Wadsworth.

Greeno, J. G. 1997. On claims that answer the wrong question. *Educational Researcher,* 26(1), 5–17.

Greeno, J. G., Smith, D. R., and Moore, J. L. 1993. Transfer of situated learning. In D. K. Detterman and R. J. Steinberg (eds.), *Transfer on trial: Intelligence, cognition, and instruction,* 99–167. Norwood, NJ: Ablex.

Griffiths, P. 1997. *What emotions really are: The problem of psychological categories.* Chicago: University of Chicago Press.

Hiebert, J., Gallimore, R., and Stigler, J. W. 1999. A knowledge base for the teaching profession: What would it look like and how can we get one? *Educational Researcher,* 31(5), 3–15.

Hirsch, E. D. 1987. *Cultural literacy: What every American needs to know.* Boston: Houghton Mifflin.

Hoetker, J., and Ahlbrand, W. P., Jr. 1969. The persistence of recitation. *American Educational Research Journal,* 6, 145–67.

hooks, b. 1994. *Teaching to transgress: Education as the practice of freedom.* New York: Routledge.

Jackson, P. W. 1968. *Life in classrooms.* New York: Holt, Rinehart and Winston.

Jagla, V. M. 1994. *Teachers' everyday use of imagination and intuition: In pursuit of the elusive image.* Albany: State University of New York Press.

James, W. 1884/1968. What is an emotion? Reproduced in M. Arnold (ed.), *The nature of emotion.* Harmondsworth, UK: Penguin.

Jenkins, J. M., and Oatley, K. 1996. *Understanding emotions.* Oxford: Blackwell.

Jersild, A. 1955. *When teachers face themselves.* New York: Teachers College Press.

Johnson, D. W. and Johnson, R. T. 2010. Energizing learning: The instructional power of conflict. *Educational Researcher,* 38(1), 37–52.

Jones, M. G., and Vesilind, E. M. 1994. Changes in student teachers' interaction with pupils. *Journal of Classroom Interaction,* 29, 25–29.

———. 1996. Putting practice into theory: Changes in the organization of preservice teachers' pedagogical knowledge. *American Educational Research Journal,* 33(1), 91–117.

Katz, M. S., Noddings, N., and Strike, K. A. (eds.). 1993. *Justice and caring: The search for common ground in education.* New York: Teachers College Press.

Kilpatrick, W. H. 1925. *Foundation of method.* New York: MacMillan.

Kincheloe, J. 2008. *Critical pedagogy,* 2nd ed. New York: Peter Lang.

Krathwohl, D. R., Bloom, B. S., and Masia, B. B. 1964. *Taxonomy of educational objectives, handbook II: The affective domain.* New York: David McKay.

Kuhn, D. 1991. *The skills of argument.* New York: Cambridge University Press.

Lacey, C. 1977. *The socialization of teachers.* London: Methuen.

Lakoff, G., and Johnson, M. 1980. *Metaphors we live by.* Chicago: University of Chicago Press.

Lampert, M. 2001. *Teaching problems and the problems of teaching.* New Haven, CT: Yale University Press

Langer, E. 1997. *The power of mindful learning.* Reading, MA: Addison-Wesley.

Lave, J., and Wenger, E. 1991. *Situated learning.* Cambridge: Cambridge University Press.

Leinhardt, G. 1990. Capturing craft knowledge in teaching. *Educational Researcher,* 19(2), 18–25.

Leinhardt, G., and Greeno, J. G. 1986. The cognitive skill of teaching. *Journal of Educational Psychology,* 78(2), 75–95.

Lewis, C., and Tsuchida, I. 1997. A lesson is like a swiftly flowing river. *American Educator* 22(4), 12–17, 50–52.

Lobato, J. 2003. How design experiments can inform a rethinking of transfer and vice versa. *Educational Researcher,* 32(1), 17–20.

Marshall, H. H. 1988. Work or learning: Implications of classroom metaphors. *Educational Researcher,* 17(9), 9–16.

Marshall, H. H., and Weinstein, R. S. 1984. Classroom factors affecting students' self-evaluations: An interactional model. *Review of Educational Research,* 54, 301–25.

Massialas, B. G., and Zevin, J. 1983. *Teaching creatively.* Malabar, FL: Kreiger.

McCaslin, M. M., and Good, T. L. 1996. *Listening in classrooms.* New York: HarperCollins.

McLuhan, M. 1967. *The medium is the message.* New York: Random House.

McNeil, L. 1986. *Contradictions of control: School structure and school knowledge.* New York: Routledge & Kegan Paul.

Meece, J. L., Blumenfeld, P. C., and Hoyle, R. H. 1988. Students' goal orientations and cognitive engagement in classroom activities. *Journal of Educational Psychology,* 80, 514–23.

Mol, S., Bus, A. G., and de Jong, M. T. 2009. Interactive book reading in early education: A tool to stimulate print knowledge as well as oral language. *Review of Educational Research,* 79(2) (June), 979–1008.

Noddings, N. 1986. *Caring: A feminist approach to ethics and moral education*. Berkeley: University of California Press.

———. 1992. *The challenge to care in schools: An alternative approach to education*. New York: Teachers College Press.

Palmer, P. 1993. *The courage to teach: Exploring the inner landscape of a teacher's life*. San Francisco: Jossey-Bass.

Parker, W. C. 1996. Curriculum for democracy. In R. Soder (ed.), *Democracy, education, and schooling*. San Francisco: Jossey-Bass.

Perkins, D. N. 1981. *The mind's best work*. Cambridge, MA: Harvard University Press.

Perrone, V. 1989. *Working papers: Reflections on teachers, schools, and community*. New York: Teachers College Press.

Peterson, P., and Clark, C. 1978. Teachers' reports of their cognitive processes during teaching. *American Educational Research Journal*, 15, 555–65.

Picard, R. 1997. *Affective computing*. Cambridge, MA: MIT Press.

Popper, K. 1972. *Objective knowledge*. London: Oxford University Press.

Putnam, R. T., and Borko, H. 1997. Teacher learning: Implications of new views of cognition. In B. U. Biddle, T. L. Good, and I. F. Goodson (eds.), *International handbook of teaching and learning*, vol. 2, 1223–96. Dordrecht, Netherlands: Kluwer.

Resnick, L. 1987. *The thinking curriculum*. Washington, DC: National Academy Press.

Resnick, L. B. 2010. Nested learning systems for the thinking curriculum. *Educational Researcher*, 39(3), 183–98.

Roby, T. W. 1988. Models of discussion. In J. T. Dillon (ed.), *Questioning and discussion: A multidisciplinary study*. Norwood, NJ: Ablex.

Rogers, E. M. 1995. *Diffusion of innovation*. New York: Free Press.

Rousseau, J.-J. 1979. *Emile*. Trans. Alan Bloom. New York: Basic Books.

Ryan, A. M., and Patrick, H. 2001. The classroom social environment and changes in adolescents' motivation and engagement during middle school. *American Educational Research Journal*, 38(2), 437–60.

Sarason, S. B. 1990. *The predictable failure of educational reform: Can we change course before it is too late?* San Francisco: Jossey-Bass.

———. 1993. *You are thinking of teaching?* San Francisco: Jossey-Bass.

———. 1999. *Teaching as a performing act*. New York: Teachers College Press.

Schneider, W., and Pressley, M. 1989. *Memory development between two and twenty*. New York: Springer-Verlag.

Schon, D. A. 1983. *The reflective practitioner: How professionals think in action*. New York: Basic Books.

Sennett, R. 1980. *Authority*. New York: Knopf.

Shulman, L. 1986. Those who understand: Knowledge growth in teaching. *Educational Researcher*, 15(7), 4–14.

Simon, H. A. 1967. Motivational and emotional controls of cognition. *Psychological Review*, 74, 29–39.

——. 1973. The structure of ill-structured problems. *Artificial Intelligence,* 4, 181–201.

Simon, K. G. 2001. *Moral questions in the classroom: How to get kids to think deeply about real life and their schoolwork.* New Haven: Yale University Press.

Skinner, B. F. 1948. *Walden Two.* New York: Macmillan.

——. 1954. The science of learning and the art of teaching. *Harvard Educational Review,* 24(2), 86–97.

Skinner, E. A., and Belmont, M. J. 1993. Motivation in the classroom: Reciprocal effects of teacher behavior and student engagement across the school year. *Journal of Educational Psychology,* 85, 571–81.

Slavin, R. E. 1990. *Cooperative learning: Theory, research, and practice.* Boston: Allyn and Bacon.

——. 1995. *Cooperative learning: Theory, research, and practice,* 2nd ed. Boston: Allyn and Bacon.

——. 2005. Evidence-based reform in education: Promise and pitfalls. *Mid-Western Educational Researcher,* 18(1), 8–13.

——. 2008. Evidence-based reform in education: Which evidence matters? *Educational Researcher,* 37(1), 47–50.

Smith, A. 1759/1984. *Theory of moral sentiments.* Indianapolis: Liberty Fund.

Smith, B. O. 1969. Toward a theory of instruction. In L. N. Nelson, *The nature of teaching.* Waltham, MA: Blaisdell.

Snow, C. E. 2001. Knowing what we know: Children, teachers, and researchers. *Educational Researcher,* 30(7), 3–9.

Soder, R. (ed.). 1996. Democracy, education, and schooling. San Francisco: Jossey-Bass.

Sternberg, R. J. 1988. *The triarchic mind: A new theory of human intelligence.* New York: Penguin Books.

Sternberg, R. J., and Grigorenko, E. L. 2000. *Teaching for successful intelligence.* Arlington Heights, IL: Skylight Professional Development.

Stigler, J. W., and Hiebert, J. 1999. *The teaching gap: Best ideas from the world's teachers for improving education in the classroom.* New York: Free Press.

Stodolsky, S., Salk, S. and Glaessner, B. 1991. Student views about learning math and social studies. *American Educational Research Journal,* 32, 227–49.

Swidler, A. 2001. *Talk of love: How culture matters.* Chicago: University of Chicago Press.

Tharp, R. G., and Gallimore, R. 1988. *Rousing minds to life: Teaching, learning, and schooling in social context.* New York: Cambridge University Press.

Tom, A. 1984. *Teaching as a moral craft.* New York: Longman.

Toulmin, S. E. 2001. *Return to reason.* Cambridge, MA: Harvard University Press.

Ullrich, W. 1985. Will and circumstance in a small group: Orientation to authority, coping/defense, and their relationship in the development of reflective student teachers. Doctoral diss., University of Wisconsin, Madison.

U.S. Department of Education. 1987. *What works: Research about teaching and learning*, 2nd ed. Washington, DC: Government Printing Office.

van Manen, M. 1991. *The tact of teaching: The meaning of pedagogical thoughtfulness*. London, ON: Althouse.

Walberg, H. J. 2000. *Effective educational practices*. Brussels: International Academy of Education.

Webb, N. M., and Palincsar, A. S. 1996. Group processes in the classroom. In D. C. Berliner and R. C. Calfee (eds.), *Handbook of educational psychology*, 841–73. New York: Simon & Schuster.

Weinstein, C. E., and Mayer, R. E. 1986. The teaching of learning strategies. In M. Wittrock (ed.), *Handbook of research on teaching*, 3rd ed., 315–27. New York: Macmillan.

Wellman, H. 1990. *The child's theory of mind*. Cambridge, MA: MIT Press.

Westerman, D. 1991. Expert and novice teacher decision-making. *Journal of Teacher Education*, 42, 292–305.

Wiggins, G. and McTighe, J. 2005. *Understanding by design*, 2nd ed. Alexandria, VA: Association for Supervision and Curriculum Development.

Wildavsky, A. 1987. *Speaking truth to power: The art and craft of policy analysis*. New Brunswick, NJ: Transaction.

Wilen, W. W. 1990. *Teaching and learning through discussion: The theory, research and practice of the discussion method*. Springfield, IL: Charles C. Thomas.

Willis, S. 1992. *Teaching thinking*. Alexandria, VA: Association for Supervision and Curriculum Development.

Wilson, S. M., Shulman, L. S., and Richert, A. 1987. 150 different ways of knowing: Representations of knowledge in teaching. In J. Calderhead (ed.), *Exploring teacher thinking*, 104–24. Sussex: Holt, Rinehart and Winston.

Wilson, S. M, with Miller, C., and Yerkes, C. 1992. Deeply rooted change: A tale of learning to teach adventurously. In J. McLaughlin et al. (eds.), *Teaching for understanding: Challenges for practice, research, and policy*, 84–129. San Francisco: Jossey-Bass.

Wise, A. 1979. *Legislated learning: The bureaucratization of the American classroom*. Berkeley: University of California Press.

Wood, K. E. 2001. *Interdisciplinary instruction: A practical guide for elementary and middle schoolteachers*, 2nd ed. Upper Saddle River, NJ: Merrill.

Zeichner, K., and Liston, D. P. 1996. *Reflective teaching*. Mahwah, NJ: Erlbaum.

About the Author

Jack Zevin is professor of education at Queens College/CUNY who began pedagogical life as a teacher on the south side of Chicago. Teaching is a passion as much as a profession for Zevin, and he has contributed many articles, books, and curricula to enhance and enrich instruction for those willing to try creative approaches inside and outside classrooms.

Breinigsville, PA USA
27 August 2010
244359BV00001B/6/P